The Irony of American History

Also by
REINHOLD NIEBUHR

THE IRONY OF
American History

REINHOLD NIEBUHR

With a new Introduction by
Andrew J. Bacevich

The University of Chicago Press
Chicago and London

The University of Chicago Press, Chicago, 60637

Copyright © 1952 by the Estate of Reinhold Niebuhr

Introduction © 2008 by Andrew J. Bacevich

All rights reserved.

First published in 1952 by Charles Scribner's Sons

University of Chicago Press edition 2008

Printed in the United States of America

17 16 15 14 13 12 11 10 09 08   1 2 3 4 5

ISBN-13: 978-0-226-58398-3 (paper)

ISBN-10: 0-226-58398-8 (paper)

Library of Congress Cataloging-in-Publication Data

Niebuhr, Reinhold, 1892–1971.

The irony of American history / Reinhold Niebuhr ; with a new introduction by Andrew J. Bacevich.

p.   cm.

"First published in 1952 by Charles Scribner's Sons."

ISBN-13: 978-0-226-58398-3 (pbk. : alk. paper)

ISBN-10: 0-226-58398-8 (pbk. : alk. paper)   1. United States—Foreign relations—20th century.   2. United States—Foreign relations—1945–1953.   3. United States—History—Philosophy.   4. United States—Civilization.   I. Title.

E744.N5 2008

973.91—dc22   2007044237

♾ The paper used in this publication meets the minimum requirements of the American National Standard for Information Sciences—Permanence of Paper for Printed Library Materials, ANSI Z39.48-1992

TO CHRISTOPHER

CONTENTS

INTRODUCTION

Andrew J. Bacevich

The times in which we live call for a Niebuhrian revival. To read Reinhold Niebuhr today is to avail oneself of a prophetic voice, speaking from the past about the past, but offering truths of enormous relevance to the present. As prophet, Niebuhr warned that what he called in this book "our dreams of managing history"— dreams borne of a peculiar combination of arrogance, hypocrisy, and self-delusion—posed a large, potentially mortal threat to the United States.[1] Today we ignore that warning at our peril.

This is all the more urgent because the management of history has emerged, since the end of the Cold War, as the all but explicitly stated purpose of American statecraft. For this reason alone the appearance of a new edition of Niebuhr's 1952 book *The Irony of American History* is cause for celebration. For it provides the master key, in my judgment, to understanding the myths and delusions that underpin this new American view of statecraft. Simply put, it is the most important book ever written on U.S. foreign policy.

————

From what perspective does Niebuhr speak to us? As pastor, teacher, activist, moral theologian, and prolific author, Reinhold Niebuhr (1892–1971) was a towering presence in American intellectual life from the 1930s through the 1960s. He was, at various points in his career, a Christian Socialist, a pacifist, an advocate of U.S. intervention in World War II, a staunch anticommunist, an architect of Cold War liberalism, and a sharp critic of the Vietnam War. As such, he defies easy categorization. Throughout his life, he viewed himself as a man of the left. Yet to classify him as a liberal or (to employ a term currently in fashion) as a progressive is to sell him short. Truth tellers transcend partisan affiliations.

Niebuhr thought deeply about the dilemmas confronting the United States as a consequence of its emergence after World War I and, even more, after World War II, as a global superpower. The truths he spoke are uncomfortable ones for us to hear—uncomfortable not only because they demand a great deal of us as citizens, but also because they outline so starkly some of our recent failures. Four such truths are especially underlined in *The Irony of American History*: the persistent sin of American Exceptionalism; the indecipherability of history; the false allure of simple solutions; and, finally, the imperative of appreciating the limits of power.

The Anglo-American colonists who settled these shores, writes Niebuhr, saw their purpose as "to make a new beginning in a corrupt world."[2] They believed "that we had been called out by God to create a new humanity."[3] They believed further that this covenant with God marked America as a new Israel.

As a Chosen People with what Niebuhr refers to as a "Messianic consciousness," Americans came to see themselves as set apart, their motives irreproachable, their actions not to be judged by standards applied to others.[4] "Every nation has its own form of spiritual pride," Niebuhr observes. "Our version is that our nation turned its back upon the vices of Europe and made a new beginning."[5] Even after World War II, he writes, the United States remained "an adolescent nation, with illusions of childlike innocency."[6] Indeed, the outcome of that war, vaulting the United States to the apex of world power, seemed to Americans to affirm that the nation enjoyed God's favor and was doing God's work.

In Niebuhr's view, America's rise to power derived less from divine favor than from good fortune combined with a fierce determination to convert that good fortune into wealth and power. The good fortune came in the form of a vast landscape, rich in resources, ripe for exploitation, and apparently insulated from the bloody cockpit of power politics.[7] The determination found expression in a strategy of commercial and territorial expansionism that proved staggeringly sucessful, evidence not of superior virtue but of shrewdness punctuated with a considerable capacity for ruthlessness.

In describing America's rise to power Niebuhr does not shrink from using words like "hegemony" and "imperialism."[8] His point is not to tag the United States with responsibility for all the world's evils. Rather, it is to suggest that it does not differ from other great powers as much as Americans may imagine.

Niebuhr has little patience for those who portray the United States as acting on God's behalf. "All men are naturally inclined to obscure the morally ambiguous element in their political cause by investing it with religious sanctity," he once observed. "This is why religion is more frequently a source of confusion than of light in the political realm." In the United States, he continued, "The tendency to equate our political with our Christian convictions causes politics to generate idolatry."[9] Evangelical conservatism and its growing influence on American politics, which Niebuhr did not live to see, have only reinforced this tendency.

Niebuhr anticipated that the American veneration of liberty could itself degenerate into a form of idolatry. In the midst of World War II, he went so far as to describe the worship of democracy as "a less vicious version of the Nazi creed." He cautioned that "no society, not even a democratic one, is great enough or good enough to make itself the final end of human existence."[10] Our prophet's skepticism on this point does not imply that he was antidemocratic. However, Niebuhr evinced an instinctive aversion to anything that smacked of utopianism, and he saw in the American Creed a susceptibility to the utopian temptation, and he suggested provocatively that "the evils against which we contend are frequently the fruits of illusions which are similar to our own."[11] Although Niebuhr was referring to the evils of communism, his comment applies equally to the present, when the United States contends against the evils of Islamic radicalism. The illusions of Osama bin Laden find their parallel in the illusions of George W. Bush. Each of these two protagonists is intent on radically

Niebuhr regarded this line of reasoning with horror. "The idea of a preventive war," he wrote "sometimes tempts minds, whose primary preoccupation is the military defense of a nation and who think it might be prudent to pick the most propitious moment for the start of what they regard as inevitable hostilities. But the rest of us must resist such ideas with every moral resource." In Niebuhr's judgment, the concept of preventive war is not only morally wrong but also stupid. "Nothing in history is inevitable," he observes, "including the probable. So long as war has not broken out, we still have the possibility of avoiding it. Those who think that there is little difference between a cold and a hot war are either knaves or fools."[17]

Throughout the second half of the twentieth century, such cautionary views, shared by many American presidents, helped to avoid a nuclear conflagration. Between 2002 and 2003, however, they did not suffice to carry the day. The knaves and fools got their war, which has yielded not the neat and tidy outcome promised, but a host of new complications.

———

The lesson is clear: it is time for Americans to give up their Messianic dreams and cease their efforts to coerce history in a particular direction. This does not imply a policy of isolationism. It does imply attending less to the world outside of our borders and more to the circumstances within. It means ratcheting down our expectations. Americans need what Niebuhr described as

changing the Middle East. Neither will succeed, but in their efforts they engage in a de facto collaboration that causes enormous mischief and suffering.

Niebuhr cherished democracy as "a method of finding proximate solutions for insoluble problems,"[12] its purpose being as much to constrain as to liberate. But for Niebuhr, the tendency to sanctify American democracy's political values and by extension U.S. policy is anathema. Today he summons us to toss aside what he calls "the halo of moral sanctity" and to disenthrall ourselves from the self-aggrandizing parable in which we cast America as liberator of the world's oppressed.

———

Why is this so important? Because it is only through self-awareness that Americans can acquire a more mature appreciation of their place in history. We must remind ourselves that "Modern man lacks the humility to accept the fact that the whole drama of history is enacted in a frame of meaning too large for human comprehension or management."[13] On this point, Niebuhr is scathing and relentless. Those who pretend to understand history's direction and ultimate destination are, in his view, charlatans or worse.

In Niebuhr's view, history is a drama in which both the story line and the dénouement remain hidden from view. The twists and turns that the plot has already taken suggest the need for modesty in forecasting what is still to come. Unfortunately, such humility is in particularly short supply in the present-day United States. Since the beginning of the Iraq War, the American government has been engaged in setting up the United States as what Niebuhr would call "tutors of mankind in its pilgrimage to perfection."[14]

After 9/11, the Bush administration announced its intention of bringing freedom and democracy to the people of the Middle East. Ideologues within the Bush administration persuaded themselves that American power, adroitly employed, could transform that region, and they intended the invasion of Iraq and the overthrow of Saddam Hussein's repressive, despotic regime to jumpstart that process. The results speak for themselves. Indeed, events have now progressed far enough to permit us to say, with Niebuhr, that in Iraq "the paths of progress" have turned out "to be more devious and unpredictable than the putative managers of history could understand."[15]

The collapse of the Bush administration's hubristic strategy for the Middle East would not have surprised our prophet. Nearly fifty years ago, he cautioned that "even the most powerful nations cannot master their own destiny." Like it or not, even great powers are subject to vast forces beyond their ability to control or even understand, "caught in a web of history in which many desires, hopes, wills, and ambitions, other than their own, are operative."[16] The masterminds who conceived the Iraq War imagined that they could sweep away the old order and usher into existence a new Iraq expected to be liberal, democratic, and aligned with the United States. Their exertions have only demonstrated how

little they understood Iraq's history—along with the dangers of playing God.

Nations possessed of outsized confidence in their own military prowess are notably susceptible to the attraction of quick and simple solutions. Americans—patience never their long suit—are by no means immune to such temptations.

In the aftermath of 9/11, an administration enamored with military might insisted on the necessity of using force to eliminate the putative threat represented by Saddam Hussein. To the Bush administration he was both an intolerable presence and an easy target. The dangers he posed were said to be growing day by day, and to delay any longer in eliminating him was, the administration said, to place at risk the nation's very survival. Besides, a war with Iraq was sure to be a "cakewalk." These were the arguments mustered in 2002 and 2003 to persuade Americans that preventive war had become necessary, justifiable, and even inviting.

A half century ago, Reinhold Niebuhr had encountered similar arguments. The frustrations of the early stalemates and hostilities in dealing with the Soviet Union, combined with knowledge of U.S. nuclear superiority to produce calls for preventive war against the U.S.S.R. In one fell swoop, advocates of this policy argued, the United States could eliminate its rival and achieve permanent peace and security.

"a sense of modesty about the virtue, wisdom and power available to us for the resolution of [history's] perplexities."[18]

Rather than engaging in vain attempts to remake the world in our own image, the United States would be better served if it focused on encouraging a stable global order, preferably one that avoids the chronic barbarism that characterized the previous century. During the run-up to the Iraq War, senior members of the Bush administration and their neoconservative supporters repeatedly expressed their disdain for mere stability. Since March 2003, they have acquired a renewed appreciation for its benefits. The education has come at considerable cost.

Niebuhr did not disdain stability. Given the competitive nature of politics and the improbability (and undesirability) of any single nation achieving genuine global dominion, he posited "a tentative equilibrium of power" as the proper goal of U.S. policy.[19] Yet he noted that efforts to establish such an equilibrium by fiat would surely fail. Creating and maintaining a balance of power require finesse and flexibility, and the nation's leaders must locate the place where national and international interests converge. This, in a nutshell, writes Niebuhr, comprises "the art of statecraft."[20]

During the Cold War, within the Western camp at least, a strategy of containment, which sought equilibrium rather than dominance, served the economic and security interests of both the United States and its allies. As a result, those allies tolerated and even endorsed American primacy. As long as Washington did not mistake leadership for a grant of arbitrary authority, the United States remained first among equals.

After 9/11, the Bush administration rejected mere equilibrium as a goal. Rather than searching for a mutually agreeable point of concurrence, President Bush insisted on calling the shots. He demanded unquestioning conformity to U.S. goals, famously declaring "you are either with us or against us." Niebuhr once observed that the wealth and power of the United States presented "special temptations to vanity and arrogance which militate against our moral prestige and authority."[21] In formulating their strategy for the so-called global war on terror, President Bush and his lieutenants succumbed to that temptation.

As a result, hitherto reliable allies have become unreliable. Washington's capacity to lead has eroded. In many parts of the world, American wealth and American power have come to seem intolerable. The Bush record represents the very inverse of what Niebuhr defined as successful statecraft.

———

This is not to suggest that restoring realism and effectiveness to U.S. foreign policy is simply a matter of reviving the habits and routines to which Washington adhered from the late 1940s through the 1980s. But many of the arguments in *The Irony of American History* apply just as well today as they did when East-West dichotomies defined foreign policy. The difficult challenges facing the United States require us to go forward, not back. And here, too, Niebuhr, speaking to us from the days of Truman and Eisenhower, offers some suggestive insights on how best to proceed.

By the time that *The Irony of American History* appeared, Niebuhr had evolved a profound appreciation for the domestic roots of U.S. foreign policy. He understood that the expansionist impulse central to the American diplomatic tradition derived in no small measure from a determination to manage the internal contradictions produced by the American way of life.

From the very founding of the Republic, American political leaders had counted on the promise and the reality of ever greater material abundance to resolve or at least alleviate those contradictions. As Niebuhr writes, "we [Americans] seek a solution for practically every problem of life in quantitative terms," convinced that more is better.[22] Through a strategy of commercial and territorial expansion, the United States accrued power and fostered material abundance at home. Expectations of ever increasing affluence in turn ameliorated social tensions and kept internal dissent within bounds, thereby permitting individual Americans to pursue their disparate notions of life, liberty, and happiness.[23] Yet even in 1952, Niebuhr expresses doubts about this strategy's long-term viability, acknowledging that expansion cannot and, he implies, *should* not "go on forever. . . ."[24]

This brings us to the nub of the matter. The positive correlations between expansionism and prosperity, or national power and individual freedom, no longer apply. The ongoing U.S. effort to transform the Greater Middle East is dissipating rather than enhancing American power. It is squandering rather than adding to our collective wealth. Rather than ensuring political freedom at home, it provides the Bush administration with pretexts to compromise our freedoms by distorting or annulling the Constitution.

Niebuhr concludes *The Irony of American History* with a memorable insight: "Should the United States perish," he writes,

> the ruthlessness of the foe would be only the secondary cause of the disaster. The primary cause would be that the strength of a giant nation was directed by eyes too blind to see all the hazards of the struggle; and the blindness would be induced not by some accident of nature or history but by hatred and vainglory.[25]

Change each "would be" to "was" and you have an inscription well suited for the memorial that will no doubt be erected one day in Washington honoring those who *have* perished—those who sacrificed their lives in Iraq.

America's stubborn unwillingness to acknowledge the truths Niebuhr describes in this little book has produced disastrous consequences, in our time and before our very eyes. To persist any longer—to indulge further the fantasy that we can force history to do our bidding—will inevitably produce even greater catastrophes. With the reappearance of this vitally important book, we won't be able to say we weren't warned.

October 1, 2007

INTRODUCTION

Notes

1. Reinhold Niebuhr, *The Irony of American History* (New York, 1952), 3.
2. *Irony of American History*, 25.
3. *Irony of American History*, 24.
4. *Irony of American History*, 69.
5. *Irony of American History*, 28.
6. *Irony of American History*, 109.
7. *Irony of American History*, 74.
8. *Irony of American History*, 110, 113.
9. D. B. Robertson, ed., *Love and Justice: Selections from the Shorter Writings of Reinhold Niebuhr* (New York, 1967), 59.
10. Reinhold Niebuhr, *The Children of Light and the Children of Darkness* (New York, 1944), 133.
11. *Irony of American History*, 16.
12. *Children of Light*, 118.
13. *Irony of American History*, 88.
14. *Irony of American History*, 71.
15. *Irony of American History*, 78.
16. Reinhold Niebuhr, *The World Crisis and American Responsibility* (New York, 1958), 81.
17. *World Crisis*, 76.
18. *Irony of American History*, 174.
19. *Beyond Tragedy*, 180.
20. *World Crisis*, 41.
21. *World Crisis*, 43.
22. *Irony of American History*, 59–60.
23. *Irony of American History*, 55.
24. *Irony of American History*, 29.
25. *Irony of American History*, p. 174.

PREFACE

The substance of this volume consists of two series of lectures. The first was given at Westminster College, Fulton, Missouri, in May 1949, under the auspices of the John Findley Green Foundation. The second was given in January 1951 at Northwestern University under the auspices of the Shaffer Lectureship. Both lectureships dealt with the position of our nation in the present world situation, as interpreted from the standpoint of the Christian faith. The Westminster and Northwestern lectures are embodied in Chapters II to VII.

The first and the last chapters, in which I seek to explain the framework of "irony" within which I have sought to interpret American history, make explicit, what was only implicit in my original lectures. Since, however, I have postponed a full exposition of the concept of "irony" as it is used in these pages to the last chapter it may be appropriate to anticipate some of the explanations of that chapter in this brief introduction.

We frequently speak of "tragic" aspects of contemporary history; and also call attention to a "pathetic" element in our present historical situation. My effort to distinguish "ironic" elements in our history from tragic and pathetic ones, does not imply the denial of tragic and pathetic aspects in our contemporary experience. It does rest upon the conviction that the ironic elements are more revealing. The three elements might be distinguished as follows: (a) Pathos is that element in an historic situation which elicits pity, but neither deserves admiration nor warrants contrition. Pathos arises from fortuitous cross-purposes and confusions in life for which no reason can be given, or guilt ascribed. Suffering caused by purely natural evil is the clearest instance of the purely pathetic. (b) The tragic element in a human situation is constituted of conscious choices of evil for the sake of good. If men or nations do evil in a good cause; if they cover themselves with guilt in order to fulfill some high responsibility; or if they sacrifice some high value for the sake of a higher or equal one they make a tragic choice. Thus the necessity of using the threat of atomic destruction as an instrument for the preservation of peace is a tragic element in our contemporary situation. Tragedy elicits admiration as well as pity because it combines nobility with

xxiii

guilt. (c) Irony consists of apparently fortuitous incongruities in life which are discovered, upon closer examination, to be not merely fortuitous. Incongruity as such is merely comic. It elicits laughter. This element of comedy is never completely eliminated from irony. But irony is something more than comedy. A comic situation is proved to be an ironic one if a hidden relation is discovered in the incongruity. If virtue becomes vice through some hidden defect in the virtue; if strength becomes weakness because of the vanity to which strength may prompt the mighty man or nation; if security is transmuted into insecurity because too much reliance is placed upon it; if wisdom becomes folly because it does not know its own limits—in all such cases the situation is ironic. The ironic situation is distinguished from a pathetic one by the fact that the person involved in it bears some responsibility for it. It is differentiated from tragedy by the fact that the responsibility is related to an unconscious weakness rather than to a conscious resolution. While a pathetic or a tragic situation is not dissolved when a person becomes conscious of his involvement in it, an ironic situation must dissolve, if men or nations are made aware of their complicity in it. Such awareness involves some realization of the hidden vanity or pretension by which comedy is turned into irony. This realization either must lead to an abatement of the pretension, which means contrition; or it leads to a desperate accentuation of the vanities to the point where irony turns into pure evil.

Our modern liberal culture, of which American civilization is such an unalloyed exemplar, is involved in many ironic refutations of its original pretensions of virtue, wisdom, and power. Insofar as communism has already elaborated some of these pretensions into noxious forms of tyranny, we are involved in the double irony of confronting evils which were distilled from illusions, not generically different from our own. Insofar as communism tries to cover the ironic contrast between its original dreams of justice and virtue and its present realities by more and more desperate efforts to prove its tyranny to be "democracy" and its imperialism to be the achievement of universal peace, it has already dissolved irony into pure evil.

Whether these concepts are fruitful principles for the interpretation of current history must be left to the reader to judge, after perusing the chapters of this volume. I must add that I have no expert competence in the field of American history; and I apologize in advance to the specialists in this field for what are undoubtedly many errors of fact and judgment. I express my gratitude to the Presidents and the committees of Westminster College and Northwestern University for many courtesies during my visits to these institutions. I am also deeply grateful to my wife, Professor Ursula Niebuhr, to Professor Edmond Cherbonnier of Barnard College, for careful reading of my manuscript and for many suggestions for its improvement and to Professor Arthur Schlesinger, Jr., of Harvard who read most of the chapters and suggested important amendments. Naturally, none of my critics must be held responsible for defects in my basic thesis or in its detailed elaboration.

REINHOLD NIEBUHR

New York City
January, 1952

CHAPTER I

*The Ironic Element in the
American Situation*

1

EVERYBODY understands the obvious meaning of the world struggle in which we are engaged. We are defending freedom against tyranny and are trying to preserve justice against a system which has, demonically, distilled injustice and cruelty out of its original promise of a higher justice. The obvious meaning is analyzed for for us in every daily journal; and the various facets of this meaning are illumined for us in every banquet and commencement-day speech. The obvious meaning is not less true for having become trite. Nevertheless it is not the whole meaning.

We also have some awareness of an element of tragedy in this struggle, which does not fit into the obvious pattern. Could there be a clearer tragic dilemma than that which faces our civilization? Though confident of its virtue, it must yet hold atomic bombs ready for use so as to prevent a possible world conflagration. It may actually make the conflict the more inevitable by this threat; and yet it cannot abandon the threat. Furthermore, if the conflict should break out, the non-communist world would be in danger of destroying itself as a moral culture in the process of defending itself physically. For no one can be sure that a war won by the use of the modern means of mass destruction would leave enough physical and social substance to rebuild a civilization among either victors or vanquished. The victors would also face the "imperial" problem of using power in global terms but from one particular center of authority, so preponderant and unchallenged that its world rule would almost certainly violate basic standards of justice.

Such a tragic dilemma is an impressive aspect of our contemporary situation. But tragic elements in present history are not as significant as the ironic ones. Pure tragedy elicits tears of admiration and pity for the hero who is willing to brave death or incur guilt for the sake of some great good. Irony however prompts some laughter and a nod of comprehension beyond the laughter; for irony involves comic absurdities which cease to be altogether absurd when fully understood. Our age is involved in irony because so many dreams of our nation have been so cruelly refuted by history. Our dreams of a pure virtue are dissolved in a situation in which it is possible to exercise the virtue of responsibility toward a community of nations only by courting the prospective guilt of the atomic bomb. And the irony is increased by the frantic efforts of some of our idealists to escape this hard reality by dreaming up schemes of an ideal world order which have no relevance to either our present dangers or our urgent duties.

Our dreams of bringing the whole of human history

2

under the control of the human will are ironically refuted by the fact that no group of idealists can easily move the pattern of history toward the desired goal of peace and justice. The recalcitrant forces in the historical drama have a power and persistence beyond our reckoning. Our own nation, always a vivid symbol of the most characteristic attitudes of a bourgeois culture, is less potent to do what it wants in the hour of its greatest strength than it was in the days of its infancy. The infant is more secure in his world than the mature man is in his wider world. The pattern of the historical drama grows more quickly than the strength of even the most powerful man or nation.

Our situation of historic frustration becomes doubly ironic through the fact that the power of recalcitrance against our fondest hopes is furnished by a demonic religio-political creed which had even simpler notions than we of finding an escape from the ambiguity of man's strength and weakness. For communism believes that it is possible for man, at a particular moment in history, to take "the leap from the realm of necessity to the realm of freedom." The cruelty of communism is partly derived from the absurd pretension that the communist movement stands on the other side of this leap and has the whole of history in its grasp. Its cruelty is partly due to the frustration of the communist overlords of history when they discover that the "logic" of history does not conform to their delineation of it. One has an uneasy feeling that some of our dreams of managing history might have resulted in similar cruelties if they had flowered into action. But there was fortunately no program to endow our elite of prospective philosopher-scientist-kings with actual political power.

Modern man's confidence in his power over historical destiny prompted the rejection of every older conception of an overruling providence in history. Modern man's confidence in his virtue caused an equally unequivocal rejection of the Christian idea of the ambiguity of human virtue. In the liberal world the evils in human nature and history were ascribed to social institutions or to ignorance or to some other manageable defect in human nature or environment. Again the communist doctrine is more explicit and therefore more dangerous. It ascribes the origin of evil to the institution of property. The abolition of this institution by communism therefore prompts the ridiculous claim of innocency for one of the vastest concentrations of power in human history. This distillation of evil from the claims of innocency is ironic enough. But the irony is increased by the fact that the so-called free world must cover itself with guilt in order to ward off the peril of communism. The final height of irony is reached by the fact that the most powerful nation in the alliance of free peoples is the United States. For every illusion of a liberal culture has achieved a special emphasis in the United States, even while its power grew to phenomenal proportions.

We were not only innocent a half century ago with the innocency of irresponsibility; but we had a religious version of our national destiny which interpreted the meaning of our nationhood as God's effort to make a new beginning in the history of mankind. Now we are immersed in world-wide responsibilities; and our weakness has

4

grown into strength. Our culture knows little of the use and the abuse of power; but we have to use power in global terms. Our idealists are divided between those who would renounce the responsibilities of power for the sake of preserving the purity of our soul and those who are ready to cover every ambiguity of good and evil in our actions by the frantic insistence that any measure taken in a good cause must be unequivocally virtuous. We take, and must continue to take, morally hazardous actions to preserve our civilization. We must exercise our power. But we ought neither to believe that a nation is capable of perfect disinterestedness in its exercise, nor become complacent about particular degrees of interest and passion which corrupt the justice by which the exercise of power is legitimatized. Communism is a vivid object lesson in the monstrous consequences of moral complacency about the relation of dubious means to supposedly good ends.

The ironic nature of our conflict with communism sometimes centers in the relation of power to justice and virtue. The communists use power without scruple because they are under the illusion that their conception of an unambiguously ideal end justifies such use. Our own culture is schizophrenic upon the subject of power. Sometimes it pretends that a liberal society is a purely rational harmony of interests. Sometimes it achieves a tolerable form of justice by a careful equilibration of the powers and vitalities of society, though it is without a conscious philosophy to justify these policies of statesmanship. Sometimes it verges on that curious combination of cynicism and idealism which characterizes communism, and is prepared to use any means without scruple to achieve its desired end.

The question of "materialism" leads to equally ironic consequences in our debate and contest with communism. The communists are consistent philosophical materialists who believe that mind is the fruit of matter; and that culture is the product of economic forces. Perhaps the communists are not as consistently materialistic in the philosophical sense as they pretend to be. For they are too Hegelian to be mechanistic materialists. They have the idea of a "dialectic" or "logic" running through both nature and history which means that a rational structure of meaning runs through the whole of reality. Despite the constant emphasis upon the "dignity of man" in our own liberal culture, its predominant naturalistic bias frequently results in views of human nature in which the dignity of man is not very clear.

It is frequently assumed that human nature can be manipulated by methods analogous to those used in physical nature. Furthermore it is generally taken for granted that the highest ends of life can be fulfilled in man's historic existence. This confidence makes for utopian visions of historical possibilities on the one hand and for rather materialistic conceptions of human ends on the other. All concepts of immortality are dismissed as the fruit of wishful thinking. This dismissal usually involves indifference toward the tension in human existence, created by the fact that "our reach is beyond our grasp," and that every sensitive individual has a relation to a structure of meaning which is never fulfilled in the vicissitudes of actual history.

The crowning irony in this debate about materialism lies in the tremendous preoccupation of our own technical culture with the problem of gaining physical security against the hazards of nature. Since our nation has carried this preoccupation to a higher degree of consistency than any other we are naturally more deeply involved in the irony. Our orators profess abhorrence of the communist creed of "materialism" but we are rather more successful practitioners of materialism as a working creed than the communists, who have failed so dismally in raising the general standards of well-being.

Meanwhile we are drawn into an'historic situation in which the paradise of our domestic security is suspended in a hell of global insecurity; and the conviction of the perfect compatibility of virtue and prosperity which we have inherited from both our Calvinist and our Jeffersonian ancestors is challenged by the cruel facts of history. For our sense of responsibility to a world community beyond our own borders is a virtue, even though it is partly derived from the prudent understanding of our own interests. But this virtue does not guarantee our ease, comfort, or prosperity. We are the poorer for the global responsibilities which we bear. And the fulfillments of our desires are mixed with frustrations and vexations.

Sometimes the irony in our historic situation is derived from the extravagant emphasis in our culture upon the value and dignity of the individual and upon individual liberty as the final value of life. Our cherished values of individualism are real enough; and we are right in preferring death to their annulment. But our exaltation of the individual involves us in some very ironic contradictions. On the one hand, our culture does not really value the individual as much as it pretends; on the other hand, if justice is to be maintained and our survival assured, we cannot make individual liberty as unqualifiedly the end of life as our ideology asserts.

A culture which is so strongly influenced by both scientific concepts and technocratic illusions is constantly tempted to annul or to obscure the unique individual. Schemes for the management of human nature usually involve denials of the "dignity of man" by their neglect of the chief source of man's dignity, namely, his essential freedom and capacity for self-determination. This denial is the more inevitable because scientific analyses of human actions and events are bound to be preoccupied with the relations of previous causes to subsequent events. Every human action ostensibly can be explained by some efficient cause or complex of causes. The realm of freedom which allows the individual to make his decision within, above and beyond the pressure of causal sequences is beyond the realm of scientific analysis. Furthermore the acknowledgment of its reality introduces an unpredictable and incalculable element into the causal sequence. It is therefore embarrassing to any scientific scheme. Hence scientific cultures are bound to incline to determinism. The various sociological determinisms are reinforced by the general report which the psychologists make of the human psyche. For they bear witness to the fact that their scientific instruments are unable to discover that integral, self-transcendent center of personality, which is in and yet above the stream of nature and time and which religion and poetry take for granted.*

8

Furthermore it is difficult for a discipline, whether philosophical or scientific, operating, as it must, with general concepts, to do justice to the tang and flavor of individual uniqueness. The unique and irreplaceable individual, with his

> Thoughts hardly to be packed
> Into a narrow act,
> Fancies that broke through language and escaped.
>
> (BROWNING)

with his private history and his own peculiar mixture of hopes and fears, may be delineated by the poet. The artist-novelist may show that his personality is not only unique but subject to infinite variation in his various encounters with other individuals; but all this has no place in a strictly scientific account of human affairs. In such accounts the individual is an embarrassment.

If the academic thought of a scientific culture tends to obscure the mystery of the individual's freedom and uniqueness, the social forms of a technical society fre-

---

*In his comprehensive empirical study of human personality Gardner Murphy nicely suggests the limits of empiricism in dealing with the self. He declares: "We do not wish to deny the possibility suggested by James Ward that all awareness is colored by selfhood. . . . Least of all do we wish to attempt to set aside the still unsolved philosophical question whether the process of experiencing necessitates the existence of a non-empirical experiencer. . . . Nothing could be gained by a Gordian-knot solution of such a tangled problem. We are concerned solely with the immediate question: Should the student of personality at the present stage of research postulate a non-empirical entity distinct from the organism and its perceptual responses? . . . To this limited question a negative answer seems advisable." Gardner Murphy, *Personality*, p. 491. There can of course be no "non-empirical entity." But there may be an entity which cannot be isolated by scientific techniques.

quently endanger the realities of his life. The mechanically contrived togetherness of our great urban centers is inimical to genuine community. For community is grounded in personal relations. In these the individual becomes most completely himself as his life enters organically into the lives of others. Thus our theory and our practice tend to stand in contradiction to our creed.

But if our academic thought frequently negates our individualistic creed, our social practice is frequently better than the creed. The justice which we have established in our society has been achieved, not by pure individualism, but by collective action. We have balanced collective social power with collective social power. In order to prevail against our communist foe we must continue to engage in vast collective ventures, subject ourselves to far-reaching national and international disciplines and we must moderate the extravagance of our theory by the soberness of our practice. Many young men, who have been assured that only the individual counts among us, have died upon foreign battlefields. We have been subjected to this ironic refutation of our cherished creed because the creed is too individualistic to measure the social dimension of human existence and too optimistic to gauge the hazards to justice which exist in every community, particularly in the international one.

It is necessary to be wiser than our creed if we would survive in the struggle against communism. But fortunately we have already been somewhat better in our practice than in our quasi-official dogma. If we had not been, we would not have as much genuine community and tolerable justice as we have actually attained. If the pre-

10

vailing ethos of a bourgeois culture also gave itself to dangerous illusions about the possibilities of managing the whole of man's historical destiny, we were fortunately and ironically saved from the evil consequences of this illusion by various factors in our culture. The illusion was partly negated by the contradictory one that human history would bear us onward and upward forever by forces inherent in it. Therefore no human resolution or contrivance would be necessary to achieve the desired goal. We were partly saved by the very force of democracy. For the freedom of democracy makes for a fortunate confusion in defining the goal toward which history should move; and the distribution of power in a democracy prevents any group of world savers from grasping after a monopoly of power.

These ironic contrasts and contradictions must be analyzed with more care presently. Our immediate prefatory concern must be the double character of our ironic experience. Contemporary history not merely offers ironic refutation of some of our early hopes and present illusions about ourselves; but the experience which furnishes the refutation is occasioned by conflict with a foe who has transmuted ideals and hopes, which we most deeply cherish, into cruel realities which we most fervently abhor.

2

One of the great works of art in the western tradition, which helped to laugh the culture of chivalry and the ideals of medieval knight errantry out of court, was Cervantes' Don Quixote. Quixote's espousal of the ideals of knighthood was an absurd imitation of those ideals; and

11

it convicted the ideals themselves of absurdity. The medieval knights had mixed Teutonic class pride and the love of adventure of a military caste with Christian conceptions of suffering love. In Quixote's imitation the love becomes genuine suffering love. Therefore, while we laugh at the illusions of this bogus knight, we finally find ourselves laughing with a profounder insight at the bogus character of knighthood itself.

Our modern civilization has similarities with the culture of medieval knighthood. But its sentimentalities and illusions are brought to judgment, not by a Christ-like but by a demonic fool; and not by an individual but a collective one. In each case a mixture of genuine idealism with worldliness is disclosed. The medieval knights mixed pride in their military prowess with pretenses of coming to the aid of the helpless. However, the helpless were not those who really needed help but some fair ladies in distress. Our modern commercial civilization mixes Christian ideals of personality, history and community with characteristic bourgeois concepts. Everything in the Christian faith which points to ultimate and transcendent possibilities is changed into simple historical achievements. The religious vision of a final realm of perfect love in which life is related to life without the coercion of power is changed into the pretension that a community, governed by prudence, using covert rather than overt forms of power, and attaining a certain harmony of balanced competitive forces, has achieved an ideal social harmony. A society in which the power factors are obscured is assumed to be a "rational" rather than coercive one. The knight of old knew about power. He sat on a horse, the symbol of military power. But the power of the modern commercial community is contained in the "counters" of stocks and bonds which are stored in the vaults of the bank. Such a community creates a culture in which nothing is officially known about power, however desperate may be the power struggles within it.

The Christian ideal of the equality of all men before God and of equality as a regulative principle of justice is made into a simple historical possibility. It is used by bourgeois man as a weapon against feudal inequality; but it is not taken seriously when the classes below him lay claim to it. Communism rediscovers the idea and gives it one further twist of consistency until it becomes a threat to society by challenging even necessary functional inequalities in the community. The Christian idea of the significance of each individual in God's sight becomes, in bourgeois civilization, the concept of a discrete individual who makes himself the final end of his own existence. The Christian idea of providence is rejected for the heady notion that man is the master of his fate and the captain of his soul.

Communism protests against the sentimentalities and illusions of the bourgeois world-view by trying a little more desperately to take them seriously and to carry them out; or by opposing them with equally absurd contradictory notions. The bourgeois world is accused of not taking the mastery of historical destiny seriously enough and of being content with the mastery of nature. To master history, declares Engels, requires a "revolutionary act." "When this act is accomplished," he insists, "—when man not only proposes but also disposes, only

13

then will the last extraneous forces reflected in religion vanish away." That is to say, man will no longer have any sense of the mystery and meaning of the drama of history beyond the limits of his will and understanding; but he will be filled with illusions about his own power and wisdom.

For the bourgeois idea of a society in which the morally embarrassing factor of power has been pushed under the rug, communism substitutes the idea of one final, resolute and unscrupulous thrust of power in the revolution. This will establish a society in which no coercive power will be necessary and the state will "wither away." The notion of a society which achieves social harmony by prudence and a nice balance of competitive interests, is challenged by communism with the strategy of raising "class antagonisms" to a final climax of civil war. In this war the proletariat will "seize the state power" and thereby "put an end to itself as a proletariat" (Engels). This is to say, it will create a society in which all class distinctions and rivalries are eliminated.

For the liberal idea of the natural goodness of all men it substitutes the idea of the exclusive virtue of the proletariat, who, according to Lenin, are alone capable of courage and disinterestedness. Thus it changes a partially harmful illusion about human nature into a totally noxious one. As if to make sure that the illusion will bear every possible evil fruit, it proposes to invest this allegedly virtuous class with precisely that total monopoly of power which is bound to be destructive of every virtue.

Communism challenges the bourgeois notion of a discrete and self-sufficing individual with the concept of a

14

society so perfect and frictionless that each individual will flower in it, and have no desires, ambitions and hopes beyond its realities. It thinks of this consummation as the real beginning of history and speaks of all previous time as "pre-history." Actually such a consummation would be the end of history; for history would lose its creative force if individuals were completely engulfed in the community. Needless to say the change of this dream into the nightmare of a coercive community, in which every form of individual initiative and conscience is suppressed, was an inevitable, rather than fortuitous, development. It proved that it is even more dangerous to understand the individual only in his social relations than to deny his social substance.

In every instance communism changes only partly dangerous sentimentalities and inconsistencies in the bourgeois ethos into consistent and totally harmful ones. Communism is thus a fierce and unscrupulous Don Quixote on a fiery horse, determined to destroy every knight and lady of civilization; and confident that this slaughter will purge the world of evil. Like Quixote, it imagines itself free of illusions; but it is actually driven by twofold ones. Here the similarity ends. In the Quixote of Cervantes the second illusion purges the first of its error and evil. In the case of the demonic Quixote the second illusion gives the first a satanic dimension.

Our own nation is both the participant and the victim of this double irony in a special way. Of all the "knights" of bourgeois culture, our castle is the most imposing and our horse the sleekest and most impressive. Our armor is the shiniest (if it is legitimate to compare atom bombs

15

with a knight's armor); and the lady of our dreams is most opulent and desirable. The lady has been turned into "prosperity." We have furthermore been persuaded by our success to formulate the creed of our civilization so passionately that we have suppressed its inconsistencies with greater consistency than any of our allies. We stand before the enemy in the first line of battle but our ideological weapons are frequently as irrelevant as were the spears of the knights, when gunpowder challenged their reign.

Our unenviable position is made the more difficult because the heat of the battle gives us neither the leisure nor the inclination to detect the irony in our own history or to profit from the discovery of the double irony between ourselves and our foe. If only we could fully understand that the evils against which we contend are frequently the fruit of illusions which are similar to our own, we might be better prepared to save a vast uncommitted world, particularly in Asia, which lies between ourselves and communism, from being engulfed by this noxious creed.

CHAPTER II

The Innocent Nation in an Innocent World

1

PRACTICALLY all schools of modern culture, whatever their differences, are united in their rejection of the Christian doctrine of original sin. This doctrine asserts the obvious fact that all men are persistently inclined to regard themselves more highly and are more assiduously concerned with their own interests than any "objective" view of their importance would warrant. Modern culture in its various forms feels certain that, if men could be sufficiently objective or disinterested to recognize the injustice of excessive self-interest, they could also in time transfer the objectivity of their judgments as observers of the human scene to their judgments as actors and agents in human history. This is an absurd notion which every practical statesman or man of affairs knows how to discount because he encounters ambitions and passions in his daily experience, which refute the regnant modern theory of potentially innocent men and nations. There is consequently a remarkable hiatus between the shrewdness of practical men of affairs and the speculations of our wise men. The latter are frequently convinced that the predicament of our possible involvement in an atomic and global conflict is due primarily to failure of the statesmen to heed the advice of our psychological and social scientists.* The statesmen on the other hand have fortunately been able to disregard the admonition of our wise men because they could still draw upon the native shrewdness of the common people who in smaller realms have had something of the same experience with human nature as the statesmen. The statesmen have not been particularly brilliant in finding solutions for our problems, all of which have reached global dimensions. But they have, at least, steered a course which still offers us minimal hope of avoiding a global conflict.

But whether or not we avoid another war, we are covered with prospective guilt. We have dreamed of a purely rational adjustment of interests in human society; and we are involved in "total" wars. We have dreamed of a "scientific" approach to all human problems; and we find that the tensions of a world-wide conflict release individual and collective emotions not easily brought under rational control. We had hoped to make neat and

---

*One of them writes: "While the scientific method has been applied wholeheartedly to everything which has to do with material advance it has been only applied haltingly and tentatively to the social and psychological problems which the advance has brought to the fore. Moreover while even the most conservative manufacturer is quick to take the advice of the chemist or engineer, the legislator rarely pays attention to the findings of the social scientist. Someone has said that in this age of wireless and airplanes the legislator typically keeps his ear to the ground." Ralph Linton in *The Science of Man in the World Crisis*, p. 219.

sharp distinctions between justice and injustice; and we discover that even the best human actions involve some guilt.

This vast involvement in guilt in a supposedly innocent world achieves a specially ironic dimension through the fact that the two leading powers engaged in the struggle are particularly innocent according to their own official myth and collective memory. The Russian-Communist pretensions of innocency and the monstrous evils which are generated from them, are the fruit of a variant of the liberal dogma. According to the liberal dogma men are excessively selfish because they lack the intelligence to consider interests other than their own. But this higher intelligence can be supplied, of course, by education. Or they are betrayed into selfishness by unfavorable social and political environment. This can be remedied by the growth of scientifically perfected social institutions.

The communist dogma is more specific. Men are corrupted by a particular social institution: the institution of property. The abolition of this institution guarantees the return of mankind to the state of original innocency which existed before the institution of property arose, a state which Engels describes as one of idyllic harmony with "no soldiers, no gendarmes, no policemen, prefects or judges, no prisons, laws or lawsuits."

The initiators of this return to innocency are the proletarian class. This class is innocent because it has no interests to defend; and it cannot become "master of the productive forces of society except by abolishing their mode of appropriation." The proletarians cannot free themselves from slavery without emancipating the whole

19

of mankind from injustice. Once this act of emancipation has been accomplished every action and event on the other side of the revolution participates in this new freedom from guilt. A revolutionary nation is guiltless because the guilt of "imperialism" has been confined to "capitalistic" nations "by definition." Thus the lust for power which enters into most individual and collective human actions, is obscured. The priest-kings of this new revolutionary state, though they wield inordinate power because they have gathered both economic and political control in the hands of a single oligarchy, are also, in theory, innocent of any evil. Their interests and those of the masses whom they control are, by definition, identical since neither owns property.

Even the vexatious and tyrannical rule of Russia over the smaller communist states is completely obscured and denied by the official theory. Hamilton Fish Armstrong reports Bukharin's interpretation of the relation of communist states to each other as follows: "Bukharin explained at length that national rivalry between Communist states was 'an impossibility by definition.' 'What creates wars,' he said, 'is the competition of monopoly capitalisms for raw materials and markets. Capitalist society is made up of selfish and competing national units and therefore is by definition a world at war. Communist society will be made up of unselfish and harmonious units and therefore will be by definition a world at peace. Just as capitalism cannot live without war, so war cannot live with Communism.' "*

It is difficult to conceive of a more implausible theory

*Hamilton Fish Armstrong, *Tito and Goliath*, p. ix.

of human nature and conduct. Yet it is one which achieves a considerable degree of plausibility, once the basic assumptions are accepted. It has been plausible enough, at any rate, to beguile millions of people, many of whom are not under the direct control of the tyranny and are therefore free to consider critical challenges of its adequacy. So powerful has been this illusory restoration of human innocency that, for all we know, the present communist oligarchs, who pursue their ends with such cruelty, may still be believers. The powers of human self-deception are seemingly endless. The communist tyrants may well legitimatize their cruelties not only to the conscience of their devotees but to their own by recourse to an official theory which proves their innocency "by definition."

John Adams in his warnings to Thomas Jefferson would seem to have had a premonition of this kind of politics. At any rate, he understood the human situation well enough to have stated a theory which comprehended what we now see in communism. "Power," he wrote, "always thinks it has a great soul and vast views beyond the comprehension of the weak; and that it is doing God's service when it is violating all His laws. Our passions, ambitions, avarice, love and resentment, etc., possess so much metaphysical subtlety and so much overpowering eloquence that they insinuate themselves into the understanding and the conscience and convert both to their party." Adams's understanding of the power of the self's passions and ambitions to corrupt the self's reason is a simple recognition of the facts of life which refute all theories, whether liberal or Marxist, about the possibility of a completely disinterested self. Adams, as every Chris-

21

tian understanding of man has done, nicely anticipated the Marxist theory of an "ideological taint" in reason when men reason about each other's affairs and arrive at conclusions about each other's virtues, interests and motives. The crowning irony of the Marxist theory of ideology is that it foolishly and self-righteously confined the source of this taint to economic interest and to a particular class. It was, therefore, incapable of recognizing all the corruptions of ambition and power which would creep inevitably into its paradise of innocency.

In any event we have to deal with a vast religious-political movement which generates more extravagant forms of political injustice and cruelty out of the pretensions of innocency than we have ever known in human history.

The liberal world which opposes this monstrous evil is filled ironically with milder forms of the same pretension. Fortunately they have not resulted in the same evils, partly because they are not as consistently held; and partly because we have not invested our ostensible "innocents" with inordinate power. Though a tremendous amount of illusion about human nature expresses itself in American culture, our political institutions contain many of the safeguards against the selfish abuse of power which our Calvinist fathers insisted upon. According to the accepted theory, our democracy owes everything to the believers in the innocency and perfectibility of man and little to the reservations about human nature which emanated from the Christianity of New England. But fortunately there are quite a few accents in our constitution which spell out the warning of John Cotton: "Let all the world give mortall man no greater power than they are content they shall use, for use it they will. . . . And they that have the liberty to speak great things you will find that they will speak great blasphemies."*

2

But these reservations of Christian realism in our culture cannot obscure the fact that, next to the Russian pretensions, we are (according to our traditional theory) the most innocent nation on earth. The irony of our situation lies in the fact that we could not be virtuous (in the sense of practicing the virtues which are implicit in meeting our vast world responsibilities) if we were really as innocent as we pretend to be. It is particularly

*From Perry Miller's *The Puritans*, p. 213.

James Bryce gives the following estimate of the philosophy which informed our constitution: "Someone has said that the American government and constitution are based on the theology of Calvin and the philosophy of Thomas Hobbes. This at least is true that there is a hearty puritanism in the view of human nature which pervades the instrument of 1787. It is the work of men who believed in original sin and were resolved to leave open for transgressors no door which they could possibly shut. . . . The aim of the constitution seems to be not so much to attain great common ends by securing a good government as to avert the evils which will flow not merely from a bad government but from any government strong enough to threaten the pre-existing communities and individual citizens." James Bryce, *The American Commonwealth*, Vol. I, p. 306.

"The doctrine of the separation of powers," declared Mr. Justice Brandeis, "was adopted by the convention of 1787 not to promote efficiency but to preclude the arbitrary exercise of power—not to avoid friction but by means of the inevitable friction incident to the distribution of governmental powers among these departments to save the people from autocracy." "Brandeis dissenting, in Myers vs. United States," 272, U. S. 52, 293.

remarkable that the two great religious-moral traditions which informed our early life—New England Calvinism and Virginian Deism and Jeffersonianism—arrive at remarkably similar conclusions about the meaning of our national character and destiny. Calvinism may have held too pessimistic views of human nature, and too mechanical views of the providential ordering of human life. But when it assessed the significance of the American experiment both its conceptions of American destiny and its appreciation of American virtue finally arrived at conclusions strikingly similar to those of Deism. Whether our nation interprets its spiritual heritage through Massachusetts or Virginia, we came into existence with the sense of being a "separated" nation, which God was using to make a new beginning for mankind. We had renounced the evils of European feudalism. We had escaped from the evils of European religious bigotry. We had found broad spaces for the satisfaction of human desires in place of the crowded Europe. Whether, as in the case of the New England theocrats, our forefathers thought of our "experiment" as primarily the creation of a new and purer church, or, as in the case of Jefferson and his coterie, they thought primarily of a new political community, they believed in either case that we had been called out by God to create a new humanity. We were God's "American Israel." Our pretensions of innocency therefore heightened the whole concept of a virtuous humanity which characterizes the culture of our era; and involve us in the ironic incongruity between our illusions and the realities which we experience. We find it almost as difficult as the communists to believe that anyone could think ill of us, since we are as persuaded as they that our society is so essentially virtuous that only malice could prompt criticism of any of our actions.

The New England conception of our virtue began as the belief that the church which had been established on our soil was purer than any church of Christendom. In Edward Johnson's *Wonder Working Providence of Zion's Saviour* (1650) the belief is expressed that "Jesus Christ had manifested his kingly office toward his churches more fully than ever yet the sons of men saw." Practically every Puritan tract contained the conviction that the Protestant Reformation reached its final culmination here. While the emphasis lay primarily upon the new purity of the church, even the Puritans envisaged a new and perfect society. Johnson further spoke of New England as the place "where the Lord would create a new heaven and a new earth, new churches and a new commonwealth together." And a century later President Stiles of Yale preached a sermon on "The United States elevated to glory and honor" in which he defined the nation as "God's American Israel."

Jefferson's conception of the innocency and virtue of the new nation was not informed by the Biblical symbolism of the New England tracts. His religious faith was a form of Christianity which had passed through the rationalism of the French Enlightenment. His sense of providence was expressed in his belief in the power of "nature's God" over the vicissitudes of history. In any event, nature's God had a very special purpose in founding this new community. The purpose was to make a new beginning in a corrupt world. Two facts about

America impressed the Jeffersonians. The one was that we had broken with tyranny. The other was that the wide economic opportunities of the new continent would prevent the emergence of those social vices which characterized the social life of an overcrowded Continent of Europe.

Jefferson was convinced that the American mind had achieved a freedom from the prejudice which corrupted the European minds, which could not be equaled in Europe in centuries. "If all the sovereigns of Europe," he declared, "were to set themselves to work to emancipate the minds of their subjects from their present ignorance and prejudice and that as zealously as they now attempt the contrary a thousand years would not place them on that high ground on which our common people are now setting out."*

One interesting aspect of these illusions of "new beginnings" in history is that they are never quite as new as is assumed, and never remain quite as pure as when they are new. Jefferson regarded the distinction between American democracy and European tyranny as an absolute one. "Under the pretense of governing," he declared in describing the European nations, "they have divided their nations into two classes, the wolves and the sheep. I can apply no milder term to the governments of Europe and to the general prey of the rich upon the poor."**
This was an understandable judgment of the state of political justice in the period of the decay of feudal society. But it was hardly a fair judgment of the potentiali-

*Writings, II, p. 249.
**Writings, VI, p. 58.

ties for democracy which were embodied in the settlement which brought William and Mary to the throne of England in 1689. It was, furthermore, generative and typical of many subsequent American judgments which obscured developments of democratic justice in Europe, particularly those which proceeded without disturbing the institution of monarchy. For monarchy remained a simple symbol of injustice to the American imagination.

The Jeffersonian poet, Freneau, used Biblical symbolism, despite his rejection of orthodox faith, to describe the significance of America's break with the traditions of tyranny. While still a student at the College of New Jersey he gave poetic expression to his faith:

> Here independent power shall hold sway
> And public virtue warm the patriot's breast.
> No traces shall remain of tyranny
> And laws and patterns for the world beside
> Be here enacted first.
> A new Jerusalem sent down from heaven
> Shall grace our happy earth.

In common with the Enlightenment Jefferson sometimes ascribed our superior virtue to our rational freedom from traditional prejudices and sometimes to the favorable social circumstances of the American Continent. "Before the establishment of the American States," he declared, "nothing was known to history but the man of the old world crowded within limits either small or overcharged and steeped in vices which the situation generates. A government adapted to such men would be one thing, but a different one for the man of these States.

27

Here every man may have land to labor for himself; or preferring the exercise of any other industry, may exact for it such compensation as not only to afford a comfortable subsistence but wherewith to provide a cessation from labor in old age."*

The illusions of a unique innocency were not confined to our earliest years. De Toqueville was made aware of them again and again on the American frontier:"If I say to an American," he reported, "that the country he lives in is a fine one, aye he replies and there is not its equal in the world. If I applaud the freedom its inhabitants enjoy he answers 'freedom is a fine thing but few nations are worthy of it.' If I remark on the purity of morals that distinguishes the United States he declares 'I can imagine that a stranger who has witnessed the corruption which prevails in other nations would be astonished at the difference.' At length I leave him to a contemplation of himself. But he returns to the charge and does not desist until he has got me to repeat all I have been saying. It is impossible to conceive of a more troublesome and garrulous patriotism."**

Every nation has its own form of spiritual pride. These examples of American self-appreciation could be matched by similar sentiments in other nations. But every nation also has its peculiar version. Our version is that our nation turned its back upon the vices of Europe and made a new beginning.

The Jeffersonian conception of virtue, had it not overstated the innocency of American social life, would have

*Writings, XIII, p. 401. (Letter to John Adams on natural aristocracy.)
**De Toqueville, American Democracy, Vol. II, p. 225.

been a tolerable prophecy of some aspects of our social history which have distinguished us from Europe. For it can hardly be denied that the fluidity of our class structure, derived from the opulence of economic opportunities, saved us from the acrimony of the class struggle in Europe, and avoided the class rebellion, which Marx could prompt in Europe but not in America. When the frontier ceased to provide for the expansion of opportunities, our superior technology created ever new frontiers for the ambitious and adventurous. In one sense the opulence of American life has served to perpetuate Jeffersonian illusions about human nature. For we have thus far sought to solve all our problems by the expansion of our economy. This expansion cannot go on forever and ultimately we must face some vexatious issues of social justice in terms which will not differ too greatly from those which the wisest nations of Europe have been forced to use.*

*On the occasion of Thomas Huxley's visit to America he made this significant prophecy: ". . . To an Englishman landing upon your shores for the first time, travelling for hundreds of miles through strings of great and well-ordered cities, seeing your enormous actual, and almost infinite potential, wealth in all commodities, and in the energy and ability which turn wealth to account, there is something sublime in the vista of the future. Do not suppose that I am pandering to what is commonly understood by national pride. I cannot say that I am in the slightest degree impressed by your bigness, or your material resources, as such. Size is not grandeur, and territory does not make a nation. The great issue, about which hangs a true sublimity, and the terror of overhanging fate, is what are you going to do with all these things? What is to be the end to which these are to be the means? You are making a novel experiment in politics on the greatest scale which the world has yet seen. Forty millions at your first centenary, it is reasonably to be expected that, at the second, these states will be occupied by two hundred millions of English-speaking people, spread over an area as large as that of Europe,

29

The idea that men would not come in conflict with one another, if the opportunities were wide enough, was partly based upon the assumption that all human desires are determinate and all human ambitions ordinate. This assumption was shared by our Jeffersonians with the French Enlightenment. "Every man," declared Tom Paine, "wishes to pursue his occupation and enjoy the fruits of his labors and the produce of his property in peace and safety and with the least possible expense. When these things are accomplished all objects for which governments ought to be established are accomplished."* The same idea underlies the Marxist conception of the difference between an "economy of scarcity" and an "economy of abundance." In an economy of abundance there is presumably no cause for rivalry. Neither Jeffersonians nor Marxists had any understanding for the perennial conflicts of power and pride which may arise on every level of "abundance" since human desires grow with the means of their gratification.

---

and with climates and interests as diverse as those of Spain and Scandinavia, England and Russia. You and your descendants have to ascertain whether this great mass will hold together under the forms of a republic, and the despotic reality of universal suffrage; whether state rights will hold out against centralisation, without separation; whether centralisation will get the better, without actual or disguised monarchy; whether shifting corruption is better than a permanent bureaucracy; and as population thickens in your great cities, and the pressure of want is felt, the gaunt spectre of pauperism will stalk among you, and communism and socialism will claim to be heard. Truly America has a great future before her; great in toil, in care, and in responsibility; great in true glory if she be guided in wisdom and righteousness; great in shame if she fail." Thomas H. Huxley, *American Addresses,* New York, D. Appleton and Co., 1877, p. 125 f.

*Thomas Paine, *The Rights of Man,* Part II, Ch. 4.

One single note of realism runs through Jefferson's idyllic picture of American innocency. That consists in his preference for an agricultural over an urban society. Jefferson was confident of the future virtue of America only in so far as it would continue as an agricultural nation. Fearing the social tensions and the subordination of man to man in a highly organized social structure, his ideal community consisted of independent freeholders, each tilling his own plot of ground and enjoying the fruits of his own labor. "Dependence begets subservience," he wrote in extolling the life of the farmer. "It suffocates the germ of virtue and prepares fit tools for the design of ambition."[*]

There is a special irony in the contrast between the course of American history toward the development of large-scale industry and Jefferson's belief that democracy was secure only in an agrarian economy. America has become what Jefferson most feared; but the moral consequences have not been as catastrophic as he anticipated. While democracy is tainted by more corruption in our great metropolitan areas than in the remainder of our political life, we have managed to achieve a tolerable justice in the collective relations of industry by balancing power against power and equilibrating the various competing social forces of society. The rise of the labor movement has been particularly important in achieving this result; for its organization of the power of the workers was necessary to produce the counter-weight to the great concentrations of economic power which justice requires.

[*]*Writings*, II, p. 229. "Those who labor in the earth," said Jefferson, "are the chosen people of God if ever he had a chosen people." *Ibid.*

We have engaged in precisely those collective actions for the sake of justice which Jefferson regarded as wholly incompatible with justice.

The ironic contrast between Jeffersonian hopes and fears for America and the actual realities is increased by the exchange of ideological weapons between the early and the later Jeffersonians. The early Jeffersonians sought to keep political power weak, discouraging both the growth of federal power in relation to the States and confining political control over economic life to the States. They feared that such power would be compounded with the economic power of the privileged and used against the less favored. Subsequently the wielders of great economic power adopted the Jeffersonian maxim that the best possible government is the least possible government. The American democracy, as every other healthy democracy, had learned to use the more equal distribution of political power, inherent in universal suffrage, as leverage against the tendency toward concentration of power in economic life. Culminating in the "New Deal," national governments, based upon an alliance of farmers, workers and middle classes, have used the power of the state to co tablish minimal standards of "welfare" in housing, social security, health services, etc. Naturally, the higher income groups benefited less from these minimal standards of justice, and paid a proportionately higher cost for them than the proponents of the measures of a "welfare state." The former, therefore, used the ideology of Jeffersonianism to counter these tendencies; while the classes in society which had Jefferson's original interest in equality discarded his ideology because they were less certain than he that complete freedom in economic relations would inevitably make for equality.

In this development the less privileged classes developed a realistic appreciation of the factor of power in social life, while the privileged classes tried to preserve the illusion of classical liberalism that power is not an important element in man's social life. They recognize the force of interest; but they continue to assume that the competition of interests will make for justice without political or moral regulation. This would be possible only if the various powers which support interest were fairly equally divided, which they never are.

Since America developed as a bourgeois society, with only remnants of the older feudal culture to inform its ethos, it naturally inclined toward the bourgeois ideology which neglects the factor of power in the human community and equates interest with rationality.

Such a society regards all social relations as essentially innocent because it believes self-interest to be inherently harmless. It is, in common with Marxism, blind to the lust for power in the motives of men; but also to the injustices which flow from the disbalances of power in the community. Both the bourgeois ideology and Marxism equate self-interest with the economic motive. The bourgeois world either regards economic desire as inherently ordinate or it hopes to hold it in check either by prudence (as in the thought of the utilitarians) or by the pressure of the self-interest of others (as in classical liberalism). Marxism, on the other hand, believes that the disbalance of power in industrial society, plus the inordinate character of the economic motive, must drive a bourgeois society to greater and greater injustice and more and more overt social conflict.

Thus the conflict between communism and the bourgeois world achieves a special virulence between the two great hegemonous nations of the respective alliances, because America is, in the eyes of communism, an exemplar of the worst form of capitalistic injustice, while it is, in its own eyes, a symbol of pure innocence and justice. This ironic situation is heightened by the fact that every free nation in alliance with us is more disposed to bring economic life under political control than our traditional theory allows. There is therefore considerable moral misunderstanding between ourselves and our allies. This represents a milder version of the contradiction between ourselves and our foes. The classes in our society, who pretend that only political power is dangerous, frequently suggest that our allies are tainted with the same corruption as that of our foes. European nations, on the other hand, frequently judge us according to our traditional theory. They fail to recognize that our actual achievements in social justice have been won by a pragmatic approach to the problems of power, which has not been less efficacious for its lack of consistent speculation upon the problems of power and justice. Our achievements in this field represent the triumph of common sense over the theories of both our business oligarchy and the speculations of those social scientists who are still striving for a "scientific" and disinterested justice. We are, in short, more virtuous than our detractors, whether foes or allies, admit, because we know ourselves to be less innocent than our theories assume. The force and danger of self-interest in human affairs are too obvious to remain long obscure to those who are not too blinded by either theory or interest to see the obvious. The relation of power to interest on the one hand, and to justice on the other, is equally obvious. In our domestic affairs we have thus builded better than we knew because we have not taken the early dreams of our peculiar innocency too seriously.

3

Our foreign policy reveals even more marked contradictions between our early illusions of innocency and the hard realities of the present day than do our domestic policies. We lived for a century not only in the illusion but in the reality of innocency in our foreign relations. We lacked the power in the first instance to become involved in the guilt of its use. As we gradually achieved power, through the economic consequences of our richly stored continent, the continental unity of our economy and the technical efficiency of our business and industrial enterprise, we sought for a time to preserve innocency by disavowing the responsibilities of power. We were, of course, never as innocent as we pretended to be, even as a child is not as innocent as is implied in the use of the child as the symbol of innocency. The surge of our infant strength over a continent, which claimed Oregon, California, Florida and Texas against any sovereignty which may have stood in our way, was not innocent. It was the expression of a will-to-power of a new community in which the land-hunger of hardy pioneers and settlers furnished the force of imperial expansion. The organs of government, whether political or military, played only a secondary role. From those early days to the present moment we have frequently been honestly deceived because our power availed itself of covert rather than overt instruments. One of the most prolific causes of delusion about power in a commerical society is that economic power is more covert than political or military power.

We believed, until the outbreak of the First World War, that there was a generic difference between us and the other nations of the world. This was proved by the difference between their power rivalries and our alleged contentment with our lot. The same President of the United States who ultimately interpreted the First World War as a crusade to "make the world safe for democracy" reacted to its first alarms with the reassuring judgment that the conflict represented trade rivalries with which we need not be concerned. We were drawn into the war by considerations of national interest, which we hardly dared to confess to ourselves. Our European critics may, however, overshoot the mark if they insist that the slogan of making "the world safe for democracy" was merely an expression of that moral cant which we seemed to have inherited from the British, only to express it with less subtlety than they. For the fact is that every nation is caught in the moral paradox of refusing to go to war unless it can be proved that the national interest is imperiled, and of continuing in the war only by proving that something much more than national interest is at stake. Our nation is not the only community of mankind which is tempted to hypocrisy. Every nation must come to terms with the fact that, though the force of collective self-interest is so great, that national policy must be based upon it; yet also the sensitive conscience recognizes that the moral obligation of the individual transcends his particular community. Loyalty to the community is therefore morally tolerable only if it includes values wider than those of the community.

More significant than our actions and interpretations in the First World War was our mood after its conclusion. Our "realists" feared that our sense of responsibility toward a nascent world community had exceeded the canons of a prudent self-interest. Our idealists, of the thirties, sought to preserve our innocence by neutrality. The main force of isolationism came from the "realists," as the slogan "America First" signifies. But the abortive effort to defy the forces of history which were both creating a potential world community and increasing the power of America beyond that of any other nation, was supported by pacifist idealists, Christian and secular, and by other visionaries who desired to preserve our innocency. They had a dim and dark understanding of the fact that power cannot be wielded without guilt, since it is never transcendent over interest, even when it tries to subject itself to universal standards and places itself under the control of a nascent world-wide community. They did not understand that the disavowal of the responsibilities of power can involve an individual or nation in even more grievous guilt.

There are two ways of denying our responsibilities to our fellowmen. The one is the way of imperialism, expressed in seeking to dominate them by our power. The other is the way of isolationism, expressed in seeking to withdraw from our responsibilities to them. Geographic circumstances and the myths of our youth rendered us more susceptible to the latter than the former temptation. This has given our national life a unique color, which is not without some moral advantages. No powerful nation in history has ever been more reluctant to acknowledge the position it has achieved in the world than we. The moral advantage lies in the fact that we do not have a strong lust of power, though we are quickly acquiring the pride of power which always accompanies its possession. Our lack of the lust of power makes the fulminations of our foes against us singularly inept. On the other hand, we have been so deluded by the concept of our innocency that we are ill prepared to deal with the temptations of power which now assail us.

The Second World War quickly dispelled the illusions of both our realists and idealists; and also proved the vanity of the hopes of the legalists who thought that rigorous neutrality laws could abort the historical tendencies which were pushing our nation into the center of the world community. We emerged from that war the most powerful nation on earth. To the surprise of our friends and critics we seemed also to have sloughed off the tendencies toward irresponsibility which had characterized us in the long armistice between the world wars. We were determined to exercise the responsibilities of our power.

The exercise of this power required us to hold back the threat of Europe's inundation by communism through the development of all kinds of instruments of mass destruction, including atomic weapons. Thus an "innocent"

38

nation finally arrives at the ironic climax of its history. It finds itself the custodian of the ultimate weapon which perfectly embodies and symbolizes the moral ambiguity of physical warfare. We could not disavow the possible use of the weapon, partly because no imperiled nation is morally able to dispense with weapons which might insure its survival. All nations, unlike some individuals, lack the capacity to prefer a noble death to a morally ambiguous survival. But we also could not renounce the weapon because the freedom or survival of our allies depended upon the threat of its use. Of this at least Mr. Winston Churchill and other Europeans have assured us. Yet if we should use it, we shall cover ourselves with a terrible guilt. We might insure our survival in a world in which it might be better not to be alive. Thus the moral predicament in which all human striving is involved has been raised to a final pitch for a culture and for a nation which thought it an easy matter to distinguish between justice and injustice and believed itself to be peculiarly innocent. In this way the perennial moral predicaments of human history have caught up with a culture which knew nothing of sin or guilt, and with a nation which seemed to be the most perfect fruit of that culture.

In this as in every other ironic situation of American history there is a footnote which accentuates the incongruity. This footnote is added by the fact that the greatness of our power is derived on the one hand from the technical efficiency of our industrial establishment and on the other from the success of our natural scientists. Yet it was assumed that science and business enterprise would insure the triumph of reason over power and passion in human history.

Naturally, a culture so confident of the possibility of resolving all incongruities in life and history was bound to make strenuous efforts to escape the tragic dilemma in which we find ourselves. These efforts fall into two categories, idealistic and realistic. The idealists naturally believe that we could escape the dilemma if we made sufficiently strenuous rational and moral efforts; if for instance we tried to establish a world government. Unfortunately the obvious necessity of integrating the global community politically does not guarantee its possibility. And all the arguments of the idealists finally rest upon a logic which derives the possibility of an achievement from its necessity. Other idealists believe that a renunciation of the use of atomic weapons would free us from the dilemma. But this is merely the old pacifist escape from the dilemma of war itself.

The realists on the other hand are inclined to argue that a good cause will hallow any weapon. They are convinced that the evils of communism are so great that we are justified in using any weapon against them. Thereby they closely approach the communist ruthlessness. The inadequacy of both types of escape from our moral dilemma proves that there is no purely moral solution for the ultimate moral issues of life; but neither is there a viable solution which disregards the moral factors. Men and nations must use their power with the purpose of making it an instrument of justice and a servant of interests broader than their own. Yet they must be ready to use it though they become aware that the power of a particular nation or individual, even when under strong religious and social sanctions, is never so used that there is a perfect coincidence between the value which justifies it and the interest of the wielder of it.

One difficulty of a nation, such as ours, which manifests itself long before we reach the ultimate dilemma of warfare with weapons of mass destruction, is that we have reached our position in the world community through forms of power which are essentially covert rather than overt. Or rather the overt military power which we wield has been directly drawn from the economic power, derived from the wealth of our natural resources and our technical efficiency. We have had little experience in the claims and counter-claims of man's social existence, either domestically or internationally. We therefore do not know social existence as an encounter between life and life, or interest with interest in which moral and non-moral factors are curiously compounded. It is therefore a weakness of our foreign policy, particularly as our business community conceives it, that we move inconsistently from policies which would overcome animosities toward us by the offer of economic assistance to policies which would destroy resistance by the use of pure military might. We can understand the neat logic of either economic reciprocity or the show of pure power. But we are mystified by the endless complexities of human motives and the varied compounds of ethnic loyalties, cultural traditions, social hopes, envies and fears which enter into the policies of nations, and which lie at the foundation of their political cohesion.

In our relations with Asia these inconsistencies are particularly baffling. We expect Asians to be grateful to us for such assistance as we have given them; and are hurt when we discover that Asians envy, rather than admire, our prosperity and regard us as imperialistic when we are "by definition" a non-imperialistic nation.

Nations are hardly capable of the spirit of forgiveness which is the final oil of harmony in all human relations and which rests upon the contrite recognition that our actions and attitudes are inevitably interpreted in a different light by our friends as well as foes than we interpret them. Yet it is necessary to acquire a measure of this spirit in the collective relations of mankind. Nations, as individuals, who are completely innocent in their own esteem, are insufferable in their human contacts. The whole world suffers from the pretensions of the communist oligarchs. Our pretensions are of a different order because they are not as consistently held. In any event, we have preserved a system of freedom in which they may be challenged. Yet our American nation, involved in its vast responsibilities, must slough off many illusions which were derived both from the experiences and the ideologies of its childhood. Otherwise either we will seek escape from responsibilities which involve unavoidable guilt, or we will be plunged into avoidable guilt by too great confidence in our virtue.

CHAPTER III

Happiness, Prosperity
and Virtue

THE Declaration of Independence assures us that "the pursuit of happiness" is one of the "inalienable rights" of mankind. While the right to its pursuit is, of course, no guarantee of its attainment, yet the philosophy which informed the Declaration, was, on the whole, as hopeful that all men, at least all American men, could attain happiness as it was certain that they had the right to pursue it. America has been, in fact, both in its own esteem and in the imagination of a considerable portion of Europe, a proof of the validity of this modern hope which reached its zenith in the Enlightenment. The hope was that the earth could be transformed from a place of misery to an abode of happiness and contentment. The philosophy which generated this hope was intent both upon eliminating the natural hazards to comfort, security and contentment; and upon reforming society so that the privileges of life would be shared equitably. The passion for justice, involved in this hope, was of a higher moral order than the ambition to overcome the natural hazards

43

to man's comfort and security. It is obviously more noble to be concerned with the pains and sorrows which arise from human cruelties and injustices than to seek after physical comfort for oneself. Nevertheless it is one of the achievements of every civilization, and the particular achievement of modern technical civilization, that it limits the natural handicaps to human happiness progressively and gives human life as much comfort and security as is consistent with the fact that man must die in the end.

All the "this-worldly" emphases of modern culture, which culminated in the American experiment, were justified protests against the kind of Christian "otherworldliness" which the "Epistle of Clement," written in the Second Century, expressed in the words: "This age and the future are two enemies . . . we cannot therefore be friends of the two but must bid farewell to the one and hold companionship with the other."

Contrary to modern secular opinion this consistent depreciation of man's historic existence does not express the genius of Christianity. In contrast to Oriental faiths it laid the foundation for the historical dynamism of the western world precisely by its emphasis upon the goodness and significance of life in history. Ideally the Christian faith strives for a balance of "a sufficient otherworldliness without fanaticism and a sufficient this-worldliness without Philistinism."*

Whether it was this ideal balance or the defeatist distortion which was challenged in Renaissance and Enlightenment, inevitably the decay of traditional and un-

---

*Friedrich von Hügel, *Eternal Life,* p. 255.

just political institutions and the remarkable success of the scientific conquest of nature unloosed the hope that all impediments to human happiness would be progressively removed. In the words of Priestley, "Nature, including both its materials and its laws, will be more at our command; men will make their situation in this world abundantly more easy and comfortable, they will prolong their existence in it and grow daily more happy. . . . Thus whatever the beginning of the world the end will be glorious and paradisiacal beyond that our imaginations can now conceive."

These hopes of the past centuries have not all been disappointed. But the irony of an age of science producing global and atomic conflicts; and an age of reason culminating in a life-and-death struggle between two forms of "scientific" politics must be admitted. This general pattern of history concerns us particularly as it is exemplified in American life and gives our American contemporary experience a peculiarly ironic savor.

The prosperity of America is legendary. Our standards of living are beyond the dreams of avarice of most of the world. We are a kind of paradise of domestic security and wealth. But we face the ironic situation that the same technical efficiency which provided our comforts has also placed us at the center of the tragic developments in world events. There are evidently limits to the achievements of science; and there are irresolvable contradictions both between prosperity and virtue, and between happiness and the "good life" which had not been anticipated in our philosophy. The discovery of these contradictions threatens our culture with despair.

45

We find it difficult to accept the threats to our "happiness" with a serenity which transcends happiness and sorrow. We are also offended by the contumely of allies as well as foes, who refuse to regard our prosperity as fruit and proof of our virtue but suggest that it may be the consequence of our vulgar Philistinism. We are therefore confronted for the first time in our life with the questions:—whether there is a simple coordination between virtue and prosperity; and whether the attainment of happiness, either through material prosperity or social peace is a simple possibility for man, whatever may be his scientific and social achievements.

1

It is difficult to isolate and do justice to the various factors which have contributed to the remarkable prosperity and the high standards of comfort of American civilization. It is even more difficult to make a true estimate of the effect of these standards upon the spiritual and cultural quality of our society. Both the Puritans and the Jeffersonians attributed the prosperity primarily to a divine providence which, as Jefferson observed, "led our forefathers, as Israel of old, out of their native land and planted them in a country flowing with all the necessaries and comforts of life." Among the many analogies which our forefathers saw between themselves and Israel was the hope that the "Promised Land" would flow with "milk and honey."

Despite the differences between the Calvinist and the Jeffersonian versions of the Christian faith, they arrived at remarkably similar conclusions, upon this as upon other issues of life. For Jefferson the favorable economic circumstances of the New Continent were the explicit purpose of the providential decree. It was from those circumstances that the virtues of the new community were to be derived. For the early Puritans the physical circumstances of life were not of basic importance. Prosperity was not, according to the Puritan creed, a primary proof or fruit of virtue. "When men do not see and own God," declared Urian Oakes (1631), "but attribute success to the sufficiency of instruments it is time for God to maintain His own right and to show that He gives and denies success according to His own good pleasure." But three elements in the situation, of which two were derived from the creed and the third from the environment gradually changed the Puritan attitude toward the expanding opportunities of American life.

The third was the fact that, once the first hardships had been endured, it became obvious that the riches of the New Continent promised remarkably high standards of well-being. These were accepted as "uncovenanted mercies." As Thomas Shepard (1605–49) put it: "To have adventured here upon the wildernesses, sorrows wee expected to have withall; though wee must confess that the Lord hath sweetened it beyond our thoughts and utmost expectations of prudent men." John Higginson, in a sermon preached to the General Court of the Massachusetts Colony in 1663 was able to assess this "sweetening" process across some successful decades. He expressed the early faith as follows: "When the Lord stirred up the spirits of so many of his people to come over into the

wilderness it was not for worldly wealth or better liveli-
hood for the outward man. The generality of the people
that came over, professed the contrary. Nor had they
any rational grounds to expect such things in such a
wilderness. Thou God hath blessed His poor people and
they have increased here from small beginnings to great
estates. That the Lord may call His whole generation to
witness. O generation see! Look upon your towns and
fields, look upon your habitations shops and ships and
behold your numerous posterity and great increase in
blessings of land and see. Have I been a wilderness to
you? We must need answer, no Lord thou hast been a
gracious God, and exceeding good unto thy servants,
even in these earthly blessings. We live in a more comfortable and plentiful manner than ever we did expect."
This is a true confession of the lack of material motives
among the first Puritans and a healthy expression of
gratitude for the unexpected material favor of the new
community. From that day to this it has remained one
of the most difficult achievements for our nation to recognize the fortuitous and the providential element in our
good fortune. If either moral pride or the spirit of rationalism tries to draw every element in an historic situation into rational coherence, and persuades us to establish
a direct congruity between our good fortune and our
virtue or our skill, we will inevitably claim more for our
contribution to our prosperity than the facts warrant.
This has remained a source of moral confusion in
American life. For, from the later Puritans to the
present day we have variously attributed American prosperity to our superior diligence, our greater skill or (more

recently) to our more fervent devotion to the ideals of freedom. We thereby have complicated our spiritual problem for the days of adversity which we are bound to experience. We have forgotten to what degree the wealth of our natural resources and the fortuitous circumstance that we conquered a continent just when the advancement of technics made it possible to organize that continent into a single political and economic unit, lay at the foundation of our prosperity.

If it is not possible for modern man to hold by faith that there is a larger meaning in the intricate patterns of history than those which his own virtues or skills supply, he would do well to emphasize fortune and caprice in his calculations. On the other hand, a simple belief in providence also does not rescue us from these perils of a false estimate of our own contributions. Of this, the course of Puritanism in our history is proof.

There were two elements in the Calvinist creed, which transmuted it from a faith which would take prosperity and adversity in its stride to a religion which became preoccupied with the prosperity of the new community. The Puritans became as enamored with it as the Jeffersonians. The latter regarded "useful knowledge" as the only valuable knowledge and defined such knowledge (to use the words of the "American Philosophical Society for the Promotion of Useful Knowledge," a focus of Jeffersonian thought) as knowledge "applied to common purposes of life, by which trade is enlarged, agriculture improved, the arts of living made more easy and comfortable and the increase and happiness of mankind promoted."

49

The one element was the emphasis upon special providence. The other element was the belief that godliness is profitable to all things, including prosperity in this life. Any grateful acceptance of God's uncovenanted mercies is easily corrupted from gratitude to self-congratulation if it is believed that providence represents not the grace of a divine power, working without immediate regard for the virtues or defects of its recipients (as illustrated by the sun shining "upon the evil and the good and the rain descending upon the just and the unjust"); but rather that it represents particular divine acts directly correlated to particular human and historical situations. Inevitably this means that providence intervenes to punish vice and to reward virtue.

Such a theory of providence means that every natural favor or catastrophe has to be made meaningful in immediate moral terms. Thus an early Puritan, Michael Wigglesworth, saw the judgment of God upon New England in the great drought of 1662. In his "God's Controversy with New England" he warned:

> This O New England has thought got by riot
> By riot and excess
> This hast thou brought upon thyself
> By pride and wantonness
> Thus must thy worldliness be whipt.
> They that too much do crave
> Provoke the Lord to take away
> Such blessings as they have.

Naturally in a community so greatly favored as the New Colony there were bound to be more signs of favor than of judgment. The theory that a divine pleasure and displeasure expressed itself in these historical vicissitudes inevitably leads to the strong conviction that our conduct must have been very meritorious. Thus confidence in "special" providence supported the belief in the complete compatibility between virtue and prosperity which characterized later Calvinist thought. William Stoughton (1631–1703) expressed it as follows in "New England's True Interest": "If any people have been lifted up to advantages and privileges we are the people. . . . We have had the eye and hand of God working everywhere for our good. Our adversaries have had their rebukes and we have had our encouragements and a wall of fire round about us."

In Calvinist thought prosperity as a mark of divine favor is closely related to the idea that it must be sought as part of a godly discipline of life. "There is no question," declared Calvin, "that riches should be the portion of the godly rather than the wicked, for godliness hath the promise in this life as well as the life to come." We are long since familiar with Max Weber's thesis in *The Protestant Ethic and the Spirit of Capitalism* that the "intra-mundane asceticism" of Calvinism was responsible for creating the standards of diligence, honesty and thrift which lie at the foundation of our capitalistic culture. Actually Weber draws some of his most significant conclusions from American evidence. He finds it particularly interesting that "capitalism remained far less developed in some of the neighbouring colonies, the later Southern States of the U. S. A., in spite of the fact that these latter were founded by large capitalists for business motives,

51

while the New England colonies were founded by preachers . . . for religious reasons."*

At any rate, the descent from Puritanism to Yankeeism in America was a fairly rapid one. Prosperity which had been sought in the service of God was now sought for its own sake. The Yankees were very appreciative of the promise in Deuteronomy: "And thou shalt do that which is right and good in the sight of the Lord: that it may be well with thee, and that thou mayest go in and possess the good land which the Lord sware unto thy fathers" (Deuteronomy 6, 18). A significant religious reservation about the relation of achievement to prosperity, which the Book of Deuteronomy also contains, was not heeded: "For the Lord thy God bringeth thee into a good land, a land of brooks of water, of fountains and depths. . . . When thou hast eaten and art full, . . . Beware that thou forget not the Lord thy God. . . . Lest when thou . . . hast built goodly houses, and dwelt therein; and when thy herds and thy flocks multiply, and thy silver and thy gold is multiplied . . . then thine heart be lifted up . . . and thou say in thine heart, My power and the might of mine hand hath gotten me this wealth" (Deuteronomy 8, 7–17).

Such religious awe before and gratitude for "unmerited" mercies was dissipated fairly early in American life. It remains the frame of our annual presidential thanksgiving proclamations, which have however contained for many years a contradictory substance within the frame. They have congratulated God on the virtues and ideals

*Max Weber, *The Protestant Ethic and the Spirit of Capitalism*, p. 55, Engl. transl.

of the American people, which have so well merited the blessings of prosperity we enjoy.

In short, our American Puritanism contributed to our prosperity by only a slightly different emphasis than Jeffersonianism. According to the Jeffersonians, prosperity and well-being should be sought as the basis of virtue. They believed that if each citizen found contentment in a justly and richly rewarded toil he would not be disposed to take advantage of his neighbor. The Puritans regarded virtue as the basis of prosperity, rather than prosperity as the basis of virtue. But in any case the fusion of these two forces created a preoccupation with the material circumstances of life which expressed a more consistent bourgeois ethos than that of even the most advanced nations of Europe.

In 1835 De Toqueville recorded his impressions of this American "this-worldliness" as it had developed from the earliest Puritanism to the "American religion" of the nineteenth century. "Not only do Americans," declared De Toqueville, "follow religion from interest but they place in this world the interest which makes them follow it. In the middle ages the clergy spoke of nothing but the future state. They hardly cared to prove that Christians may be happy here below. But American preachers are constantly referring to the earth. . . . To touch their congregations they always show them how favorable religious opinion is to freedom and public tranquillity; and it is often difficult to ascertain from their discourses whether the principal object of religion is to obtain eternal felicity or prosperity in this world."*

*De Toqueville, *Democracy in America*, Vol. II, p. 127.

Perhaps one of the difficulties of this problem is exhibited in De Toqueville's own contrast between "eternal felicity" and "prosperity in this world." The real choice does not lie between religions which promise future bliss at the expense of indifference toward the joys and sorrows of our present life; and those which are concerned with material security and comfort. The real question is whether a religion or a culture is capable of interpreting life in a dimension sufficiently profound to understand and anticipate the sorrows and pains which may result from a virtuous regard for our responsibilities; and to achieve a serenity within sorrow and pain which is something less but also something more than "happiness." Our difficulty as a nation is that we must now learn that prosperity is not simply coordinated to virtue, that virtue is not simply coordinated to historic destiny and that happiness is no simple possibility of human existence.

2

There is an ironic aspect in the communist indictment of a religious culture, particularly when applied to America. According to communism, religion is a consolation for weak hearts who have failed to master life's "extraneous forces." It will vanish away when man learns not only to "propose" but to "dispose" over "the extraneous forces which control men's daily lives." Actually all the healthy western nations who have managed to throw off the poison of communism have been prompted by both religious and secular motives to conquer nature and reform society in the interest of man's comfort and security. They have succeeded rather better than communism in bringing "abundance" to the people. They have erred not so much in despising the comforts of this life as in promising men more comfort in life than can be fulfilled, particularly since the same technics which provide the comfort also create the weapons by which the enmity between ourselves and our brothers is sharpened.

Consideration of the American cult of prosperity cannot be dismissed without viewing one additional facet of the phenomenon. If the alleged preoccupation of the American people with living standards is primarily derived from the breadth of opportunity on a new continent and from Calvinist and Jeffersonian conceptions of religion and virtue, it also has other, less observed, roots. It is Spengler's thesis that the extravert interests, related to the scientific, technical and social problems of a civilization, are released when the death of a culture has chilled the intravert interests, which create philosophical, religious and æsthetic disciplines. Thus American "go-getting" would be related to the flowering of Western European civilization as Roman bridge and road building was related to the spring-and-summer-time of Græco-Roman culture. In each case it represents the winter of decay. De Toqueville suggests a similar thesis in his observations of American life, when he contrasts the extravert activities of our "democracy" with the purer culture of the more traditional world. "A democratic state of society," he declared, "keeps the greater part of man in a constant state of activity; and the habits of mind which are suited for the active life are not always suited for a contemplative one. . . . The greater part of men who constitute these (the democratic) nations are extremely eager in the pursuit of actual and physical gratification. As they are always dissatisfied with the position which they occupy and are always free to leave it, they think of nothing but the means of changing their fortune or increasing it."*

In ascribing preoccupation with the material basis of life to democracy De Toqueville may not do justice to all aspects of the issue, but he does place his finger upon an unsolved problem of our democracy. For it is certainly the character of our particular democracy, founded on a vast continent, expanding as a culture with its expanding frontier and creating new frontiers of opportunity when the old geographic frontiers were ended, that every ethical and social problem of a just distribution of the privileges of life is solved by so enlarging the privileges that either an equitable distribution is made easier, or a lack of equity is rendered less noticeable. For in this abundance the least privileged members of the community are still privileged, compared with less favored communities. No democratic community has followed this technique of social adjustment more consistently than we. No other community had the resources to do so. It would be quite unjust to make a purely cynical estimate of this achievement. For the achievement includes recognition by American capitalists (what French capitalists, for instance, have not learned) that high wages for workers make mass production efficiency possible. Perhaps it ought to be added that this insight was not a purely rational achievement. It was forced upon the industrialists by the pressure of organized labor; but they learned to accept the policy of high wages as not detrimental to their own in-

*Ibid., pp. 42–45.

terests somewhat in the same fashion as monarchists learned the value of constitutional monarchy, after historic pressures had destroyed the institution of monarchy in its old form.

Yet the price which American culture has paid for this amelioration of social tensions through constantly expanding production has been considerable. It has created moral illusions about the ease with which the adjustment of interests to interests can be made in human society. These have imparted a quality of sentimentality to both our religious and our secular, social and political theories. It has also created a culture which makes "living standards" the final norm of the good life and which regards the perfection of techniques as the guarantor of every cultural as well as of every social-moral value.

3

The progress of American culture toward hegemony in the world community as well as toward the ultimate in standards of living has brought us everywhere to limits where our ideals and norms are brought under ironic indictment. Our confidence in the simple compatibility between prosperity and virtue is challenged particularly in our relations with Asia; for the Asians, barely emerging from the desperate poverty of an agrarian economy, are inclined to regard our prosperity as evidence of our injustice. Our confidence in the compatibility between our technical efficiency and our culture is challenged, particularly in our relations with Europe. For the European nations, France especially, find our culture "vulgar," and pretend to be imperiled by the inroads of an American synthetic drink upon the popularity of their celebrated wines. The French protest against "Cocacolonialism" expresses this ironic conflict in a nutshell. Our confidence in happiness as the end of life, and in prosperity as the basis of happiness is challenged by every duty and sacrifice, every wound and anxiety which our world-wide responsibilities bring upon us.

The cultural aversion of France toward us expresses explicitly what most of Europe seems to feel. In its most pessimistic moods European neutralism charges, in the words of *Le Monde,* that we are a "technocracy" not too sharply distinguished from the Russian attempt to bring all of life under technical control. It is doubly ironic that this charge should be made against us by France. Europe accuses us of errors of which the whole of modern bourgeois society is guilty and which we merely developed more consistently than European nations; for the cult of technical efficiency was elaborated among us without the checks which the ethos of a traditional aristocratic culture provided in Europe. On the other hand, there is a measure of truth in the charge of similarity between our culture and that of the pure Marxists because both are offshoots of the ethos which had its rise, significantly, in the same France which is now our principal critic in Europe. Marxism transmutes every illusion of a technical society into an obvious corruption by giving a monopoly of power to an elite, who desires to remold life within terms of the simple limits which it has set for life's meaning. Against such corruptions our democratic society offers guarantees, and prevents the consistent application

58

of standards of technical efficiency to all the ends and purposes of life.

But it cannot be denied that a bourgeois society is in the process of experiencing the law of diminishing returns in the relation of technics and efficiency to the cultural life. The pursuit of culture requires certain margins of physical security and comfort; but the extension of the margins does not guarantee the further development of cultural values. It may lead to a preoccupation with the margins and obsession with the creature comforts. The elaboration of technics is basic to the advancement of culture. The inventions of writing and printing represent two of the most important chapters in the history of culture. But the further elaboration of communications in the arts of mass communication have led to the vulgarization of culture as well as to the dissemination of its richest prizes among the general public. Television may represent a threat to our culture analogous to the threat of atomic weapons to our civilization. America is the home of Hollywood in the imagination of Europe; though Europe hardly makes a fair appraisal of the relative involvement of producer and consumer in the purveyance of vulgar or sentimental art, holding us responsible for the production of what its millions avidly consume. In this, as in other respects, we must discount some of the European criticisms. Europe's belief that a nation as fortunate as our own could not possibly also possess and appreciate the nobler values of life may sometimes hide frustrated desire.

Yet we cannot deny the indictment that we seek a solution for practically every problem of life in quantitative terms; and are not fully aware of the limits of this approach. The constant multiplication of our high school and college enrollments has not had the effect of making us the most "intelligent" nation, whether we measure intelligence in terms of social wisdom, æsthetic discrimination, spiritual serenity or any other basic human achievement. It may have made us technically the most proficient nation, thereby proving that technical efficiency is more easily achieved in purely quantitative terms than any other value of culture.

Our preoccupation with technics has had an obviously deleterious effect upon at least one specific sector of our classical cultural inheritance. No national culture has been as assiduous as our own in trying to press the wisdom of the social and political sciences, indeed of all the humanities, into the limits of the natural sciences. The consequence of this effort must be analyzed more carefully in another context. It is worth noting here that, when political science is severed from its ancient rootage in the humanities and "enriched" by the wisdom of sociologists, psychologists and anthropologists, the result is frequently a preoccupation with minutiæ which obscures the grand and tragic outlines of contemporary history, and offers vapid solutions for profound problems. Who can deny the irony of the contrast between the careful study of human "aggressiveness" in our socio-psychological sciences, and our encounter with a form of aggressiveness in actual life which is informed by such manias, illusions, historic aberrations and confusions, as could not possibly come under the microscope of the scientific procedures used in some of these studies?

60

4

Happiness is desired by all men; and moments of it are probably attained by most men. Only moments of it can be attained because happiness is the inner concomitant of neat harmonies of body, spirit and society; and these neat harmonies are bound to be infrequent. There is no simple harmony between our ambitions and achievements because all ambitions tend to outrun achievements. There is no neat harmony between the conscious ends of life and the physical instruments for its attainment; for the health of the body is frail and uncertain. "Brother Ass" always fails us at some time; and, in any event, he finally perishes. There is no neat harmony between personal desires and ambitions and the ends of human societies no matter how frantically we insist with the eighteenth century that communities are created only for the individual. Communities, cultures and civilizations are subject to perils which must be warded off by individuals who may lose their life in the process. There are many young American men in Korea today who have been promised the "pursuit of happiness" as an inalienable right. But the possession of the right brings them no simple happiness. Such happiness as they achieve is curiously mixed with pain, anxiety and sorrow. It is in fact not happiness at all. If it is anything, it may be what Lincoln called "the solemn joy that must be yours to have laid so costly a sacrifice upon the altar of freedom."

There is no simple congruity between the ideals of sensitive individuals and the moral mediocrity of even the best society. The liberal hope of a harmonious "adjustment" between the individual and the community is a more vapid and less dangerous hope that the communist confidence in a frictionless society in which all individual hopes and ideals are perfectly fulfilled. The simple fact is that an individual rises indeterminately above every community of which he is a part. The concept of "the value and dignity of the individual" of which our modern culture has made so much is finally meaningful only in a religious dimension. It is constantly threatened by the same culture which wants to guarantee it. It is threatened whenever it is assumed that individual desires, hopes and ideals can be fitted with frictionless harmony into the collective purposes of man. The individual is not discrete. He cannot find his fulfillment outside of the community; but he also cannot find fulfillment completely within society. In so far as he finds fulfillment within society he must abate his individual ambitions. He must "die to self" if he would truly live. In so far as he finds fulfillment beyond every historic community he lives his life in painful tension with even the best community, sometimes achieving standards of conduct which defy the standards of the community with a resolute "we must obey God rather than man." Sometimes he is involved vicariously in the guilt of the community when he would fain live a life of innocency. He will possibly man a bombing plane and suffer the conscience pricks of the damned that the community might survive.

There are no simple congruities in life or history. The cult of happiness erroneously assumes them. It is possible to soften the incongruities of life endlessly by the scientific conquest of nature's caprices, and the social and political triumph over historic injustice. But all such strategies cannot finally overcome the fragmentary character of human existence. The final wisdom of life requires, not the annulment of incongruity but the achievement of serenity within and above it.

Nothing that is worth doing can be achieved in our lifetime; therefore we must be saved by hope. Nothing which is true or beautiful or good makes complete sense in any immediate context of history; therefore we must be saved by faith. Nothing we do, however virtuous, can be accomplished alone; therefore we are saved by love. No virtuous act is quite as virtuous from the standpoint of our friend or foe as it is from our standpoint. Therefore we must be saved by the final form of love which is forgiveness.

The irony of America's quest for happiness lies in the fact that she succeeded more obviously than any other nation in making life "comfortable," only finally to run into larger incongruities of human destiny by the same achievements by which it escaped the smaller ones. Thus we tried too simply to make sense out of life, striving for harmonies between man and nature and man and society and man and his ultimate destiny, which have provisional but no ultimate validity. Our very success in this enterprise has hastened the exposure of its final limits. Over these exertions we discern by faith the ironical laughter of the divine source and end of all things. "He that sitteth in the heavens shall laugh" (Psalm 2, 4). He laughs because "the people imagine a vain thing." The scripture assures us that God's laughter is derisive, having the sting of judgment upon our vanities in it. But if the laughter is truly ironic it must symbolize mercy as well as judgment. For whenever judgment defines the limits of human striving it creates the possibility of an humble acceptance of those limits. Within that humility mercy and peace find a lodging place.

CHAPTER IV

The Master of Destiny

1

THE communist movement against which the whole world must now stand on guard was intended as a scheme for giving man complete control of his own destiny. The supposed evils of its "materialism" and its "atheism" are insignificant compared with the cruelties which follow inevitably from the communist pretension that its elite has taken "the leap from the realm of necessity to the realm of freedom," and is therefore no longer subject to the limitations of nature and history which have hitherto bound the actions of men. It imagines itself the master of historical destiny. Some of the cruelty of the communist elite arises inevitably from the delusions of grandeur in such a conception. Some is the consequence of the fury of frustration when the supposed masters of history are confronted and opposed by recalcitrant forces in history. These have not conformed to the communist logic; their strength has not been sapped by their "inner contradictions" and they have not been forced to capitulate to communist power.

The "realm of freedom," which according to communist thought is achieved when the proletariat acts under the guidance of the party to overturn the old order, is not the freedom of the individual in society. It is the freedom of man *per se*. Of course, man *per se* does not easily act with a single mind or will. But the logic of history has given the "working class" a very special position in the historical process, because "they cannot become masters of the productive forces of society except by abolishing their own previous mode of appropriation. . . . All previous movements were movements of minorities. The proletarian movement is the self-conscious movement of the immense majority" which cannot act without acting for the whole of mankind, which "cannot stir, cannot raise itself without the whole superincumbent strata of society being sprung into the air" (*Communist Manifesto*). This class, which is potentially mankind itself, does, however, require tutelage. Without the aid of its "vanguard," the party, it would not, according to Lenin, rise above "trade union psychology." That is to say, it would be content to pursue moderate and proximate goals in history. It requires the wisdom of the party, repository of the oracles of God (in this case the wisdom of "Marxist-Leninist science") to understand the grand strategy of a secularized providence which has marked it out for so momentous a task and for so remarkable a triumph.

This whole conception has, as many observers have remarked, the character of religious apocalypse. But it is a very modern kind of religious apocalypse; for it contains the dearest hope of all typical moderns, Marxist or non-Marxist. That hope is that man may be delivered from his ambiguous position of being both creature and creator of the historical process and become unequivocally the master of his own destiny. The Marxist dream is distinguished from the liberal dream by a sharper and more precise definition of the elite which is to act as surrogate for mankind, by more specific schemes for endowing this elite with actual political power; by its fanatic certainty that it knows the end toward which history must move; and by its consequent readiness to sacrifice every value of life for the achievement of this end. The liberal culture has been informed by similar hopes since the eighteenth century. It has been as impatient as Marxism with the seeming limitations of human wisdom in discerning the total pattern of destiny in which human actions take place, and the failure of human power to bring the total pattern under the dominion of the human will. "If man can predict with almost complete certainty," asked Condorcet, "the phenomena of which he knows the laws, if . . . from the experience of the past he can forecast with much probability the events of the future, why should one regard it as a chimerical undertaking to trace with some likeness the future destiny of the human species in accordance with the facts of history?" Condorcet was not only certain that the future could be known but that he knew it. "Our hopes for the future state of the human species," he continued, "may be reduced to three important points: the destruction of inequality between nations, the progress of equality among the common people, and the growth of man toward perfection" required no more than that "the vast distance which divides the most enlightened people . . . such as the French and

Anglo-Americans" from those people who are "in servitude to kings" should "gradually disappear."*

Obviously the idea of the abolition of the institution of monarchy as the most important strategy for the redemption of mankind was as characteristic of the peculiar prejudices of middle-class life as the idea of the abolition of the institution of property was of the unique viewpoint of propertyless proletarians. In each case they identified all evil with the type of power from which they suffered and which they did not control; and they regarded particular sources of particular social evils as the final source of all evil in history. Neither Condorcet, nor Comte in his subsequent elaborations of similar hopes, placed all their trust in this single strategy. The liberal world has always oscillated between the hope of creating perfect men by eliminating the social sources of evil and the hope of so purifying human "reason" by educational techniques that all social institutions would gradually become the bearers of a universal human will, informed by a universal human mind. These ambiguities, which have saved the Messianic dreams of the liberal culture from breeding the cruelties of communism, must be considered more fully presently. At the moment it is worth recording that the Frenchman, Condorcet, envisaged the French and the "Anglo-Americans" as the Messianic nations. Here we have in embryo what has become the ironic situation of our own day. The French Enlightenment consistently saw the American Revolution and the founding of the new American nation as a harbinger of the perfect world which was in the making. Though Comte, almost

*Condorcet, *Dixième Époque*, p. 236.

a century later, rigorously clung to the idea of French hegemony in the coming utopia and fondly hoped that French would be its universal language, France has fallen by the wayside as a nation with a Messianic consciousness, its present mood being characterized by extreme skepticism rather than apocalyptic hopes.

This leaves America as the prime bearer of this hope and dream. From the earliest days of its history to the present moment, there is a deep layer of Messianic consciousness in the mind of America. We never dreamed that we would have as much political power as we possess today; nor for that matter did we anticipate that the most powerful nation on earth would suffer such an ironic refutation of its dreams of mastering history. For our increased power related our will and purpose to a vaster and vaster entanglement with other wills and purposes, which made it impossible for any single will to prevail or any specific human goal of history easily to become the goal of all mankind.

We were, as a matter of fact, always vague, as the whole liberal culture is fortunately vague, about how power is to be related to the allegedly universal values which we hold in trust for mankind. We were, of course, not immune to the temptation of believing that the universal validity of what we held in trust justified our use of power to establish it. Thus in the debate on the annexation of Oregon, in which the imperial impulse of a youthful nation expressed itself, a Congressman could thunder: "If ours is to be the home of the oppressed, we must extend our territory in latitude and longitude to the demand of the millions which are to follow us; as well for our own posterity as for those who are invited to our peaceful shores to partake in our republican institutions."

Generally, however, the legitimization of power was not the purpose of our Messianic consciousness. We felt that by example and by unexplained forces in history our dream would become the regnant reality of history.

We have noted in another connection that in both the Calvinist and the Jeffersonian concept of our national destiny the emphasis lay at the beginning upon providence rather than human power. Jefferson had proposed for the seal of the United States a picture of "the children of Israel, led by a cloud by day and a pillar of fire by night." Washington declared in his first inaugural that "the preservation of the sacred fire of liberty and the destiny of the republican model of government are justly considered, perhaps as deeply, as finally staked on the experiment intrusted to the hands of the American people." Most significant was the assurance that we were acting as surrogates, as trustees for mankind. As Dr. Priestley put it in 1802: "It is impossible not to be sensible that we are acting for all mankind."

This concept of America as the darling of divine providence did not, of course exclude the idea of fulfilling its destiny by actions which would help in the universal realization of the democratic ideal of society. The Puritans, as we have seen, gradually shifted from their emphasis upon a divine favor to the nation, to an emphasis upon the virtue which the nation had acquired by divine favor. Even a very early Puritan was certain that "God had sifted a whole nation that he might send choice

70

grain into the wilderness" (William Stoughton, 1668).

President Johnson in his message to Congress in 1868 expressed the most popular form of our Messianic dream. "The conviction is rapidly gaining ground in the American mind," he declared, "that with increased facilities for inter-communication between all portions of the earth the principles of free government as embraced in our constitution . . . would prove sufficient strength and breadth to comprehend within their sphere and influence the civilized nations of the world." Except in moments of aberration we do not think of ourselves as the potential masters, but as tutors of mankind in its pilgrimage to perfection.

Such Messianic dreams, though fortunately not corrupted by the lust of power, are of course not free of the moral pride which creates a hazard to their realization. "God has not been preparing the English-speaking and Teutonic peoples," declared Senator Beveridge of Indiana, "for a thousand years for nothing but vain and idle self-contemplation and self-admiration. He has made us the master organizers of the world to establish system where chaos reigns. . . . He has made us adept in government that we may administer government among savage and senile peoples. Were it not for such a force this world would relapse into barbarism and night. And of all our race he has marked the American people as his chosen nation to finally lead in the regeneration of the world." The concept of administering "government among savage and senile peoples" does of course have power implications. But the legitimization of power is generally subordinate in the American dream to the fact that the concept that a divine favor upon the nation implies a commitment "to lead in the regeneration of mankind." Among us, as well as among communists, an excessive voluntarism which finally brings human history under the control of the human will is in tentative, but not in final, contradiction to a determinism which finds historical destiny favorable at some particular point to man's assumption of mastery over that destiny. The American dream is not particularly unique. Almost every nation has had a version of it.*

But the American experience represents a particularly unique and ironic refutation of the illusion in all such dreams. The illusions about the possibility of managing historical destiny from any particular standpoint in history, always involve, as already noted, miscalculations about both the power and the wisdom of the managers and of the weakness and the manageability of the historical "stuff" which is to be managed.

2

Consistent with the general liberal hope of redeeming history, the American Messianic dream is vague about the political or other power which would be required to subject all recalcitrant wills to the one will which is informed by the true vision. We have noted that much of

*See Lionel Curtis' *Civitas Dei* for the British version. Fichte had a vision of the German nation becoming a *Menschheitsnation*. Mazzini artfully combined national pride with the hope of Italy's peculiar contribution to the development of mankind. Russia has always been filled with Messianic illusions. In Nicholas Berdyaev's posthumously published *The Russian Idea*, he analyzes these Messianic illusions humorously and comes to the conclusion that the Soviet Messianism is not an ideal but yet a tolerable culmination of all these Messianic dreams.

the virulence of communism arises from the fact that its program provides for the investment of a class and a party with a monopoly of power. According to the communist creed this monopoly is achieved by a remarkable concurrence between providence and the resolute will of the proletariat. Providence (*i.e.,* the historical dialectic) insures the progressive weakening of the "expropriators" and the strengthening of the "expropriated"; but, at a final climax of history, human action must support and affirm the historical logic. The proletariat must seize all political power and deny it to all of its enemies. This monopoly of power, which is to insure the victory of justice, actually becomes the root of the cruelty and injustice of communism.

In the liberal versions of the dream of managing history, the problem of power is never fully elaborated. Beginning with the physiocrats one version of the dream assumes that history would flow inevitably to the goal of an ideal humanity, if only the irrelevancies of political power were removed. But another version of the dream assumes some kind of elite. Beginning with Comte modern social scientists and geneticists frequently hint vaguely at the necessity of Platonic philosopher-kings, transmuted, of course, into scientist-kings. The least that seems required is that the men of power should have social and psychological scientists at their elbows to prevent "irrational prejudices" from entering into their calculations and to persuade them not "to have their ears to the ground." But there is, of course, no political program for investing an elite with power.

The American national version of the dream had this

73

same fortunate vagueness. American government is regarded as the final and universally valid form of political organization. But, on the whole, it is expected to gain its ends by moral attraction and imitation. Only occasionally does an hysterical statesman suggest that we must increase our power and use it in order to gain the ideal ends, of which providence has made us the trustees.

The first element of irony lies in the fact that our nation has, without particularly seeking it, acquired a greater degree of power than any other nation of history. The same technics, proficiency in the use of which lies at the foundation of American power, have created a "global" political situation in which the responsible use of this power has become a condition of survival of the free world. It is not surprising that the communist elite should be filled with fury when they behold the unfolding of this power, marked by their "logic" for self-destruction through its "inner contradictions."

But the second element of irony lies in the fact that a strong America is less completely master of its own destiny than was a comparatively weak America, rocking in the cradle of its continental security and serene in its infant innocence. The same strength which has extended our power beyond a continent has also interwoven our destiny with the destiny of many peoples and brought us into a vast webb of history in which other wills, running in oblique or contrasting directions to our own, inevitably hinder or contradict what we most fervently desire. We cannot simply have our way, not even when we believe our way to have the "happiness of mankind" as its promise. Even in the greatness of our power we are thwarted by a ruthless foe, who is ironically the more recalcitrant and ruthless because his will is informed by an impossible dream of bringing happiness to all men if only he can eliminate our recalcitrance.

But we are thwarted by friends and allies as well as by foes. Our dream of the universal good is sufficiently valid to bring us in voluntary alliance with many peoples, who have similar conceptions of the good life. But neither their conceptions of the good, nor their interests, which are always compounded with ideals, are identical with our own. In this situation it is natural that many of our people should fail to perceive that historical destiny may be beguiled, deflected and transfigured by human policy, but that it cannot be coerced. They become impatient and want to use the atomic bomb (symbol of the technical efficiency upon which our world authority rests) not only to put an end to the recalcitrance of our foes but to eliminate the equivocal attitudes of the Asian and other peoples, who are not as clearly our allies as we should like them to be. Yet on the whole, we have as a nation learned the lesson of history tolerably well. We have heeded the warning "let not the wise man glory in his wisdom, let not the mighty man glory in his strength." Though we are not without vainglorious delusions in regard to our power, we are saved by a certain grace inherent in common sense rather than in abstract theories from attempting to cut through the vast ambiguities of our historic situation and thereby bringing our destiny to a tragic conclusion by seeking to bring it to a neat and logical one.

Significantly the elements in our population which are most prone to defy the limits of power, possessed by any particular agent in history, and to seek a resolution of our difficulties by a sheer display of military power, are frequently drawn from a bourgeois-liberal tradition which was, until recently, unconscious of the factor of power in political life. It is the nature of a business community that it deals with the covert forms of power in economic life and to be insensible to the significance and the complexity of more overt forms of power, even as it is insensible to the motive of the lust for power as an element in human nature. It is quite conscious of the force of self-interest in life; but it imagines that this force is nicely checked and contained by prudence on the one hand and by the balance of competing interests on the other. The realm of the political with its vast imponderables of power is a *terra incognita* to it. When experience suddenly thrusts the facts and perils of this world upon it, it is inclined to exchange the sentimentalities and pretensions of yesterday, which obscured the power element in life, for the cynicism of today. This is the greater temptation for elements in the American business community because American world authority rests so directly upon our military power; and this in turn is drawn so immediately from our economic strength. We have had so little experience in managing or participating in the conscious and quasi-conscious power struggles of life and in fathoming the endlessly complex compounds of ethnic loyalties, historic traditions, military strength and ideological hopes which constitute historic forms of power, that we would fain move with one direct leap from the use of economic to the use of military power. These are the political and moral hazards of a great commercial nation, moving directly and precipitately into the baffling currents of world politics. Despite the hazards, we have managed to achieve some patience and shrewdness and have avoided the ultimate error of trying to bring the historic process to what would seem to us to be its ultimate conclusion.

3

If the democratic world has refused, with an unconscious or inherited wisdom, to invest its supposed elite with a monopoly of power it has not been equally wise in understanding the limits of wisdom among any supposed bearers of the Messianic vision, or in anticipating the illogical and unpredictable emergence of wisdom and virtue among those who are supposed to be the beneficiaries, rather than the benefactors, of the management of historical destiny. In this lesson the course of American history is a neat and ironic parable for the whole meaning of the liberal dream. How pure our democratic virtue seemed in the eighteenth century, compared with that of the benighted devotees and victims of "monarchy." That is why our American experiment seemed to be the "last best hope of mankind." That is why our founding fathers regarded our constitution as a veritable ark of the covenant of democracy.

But meanwhile there were many more thousands in Europe who had not "bowed their knees to Baal" than our American Elijah imagined. The hated institution of monarchy was gradually brought under parliamentary control by the rising power of democracy in Europe. The combination of constitutional monarchy and parliamentary government has proved to possess some democratic virtues which the system of checks and balances in our republican government lacks. The institution of monarchy, shorn of its absolute power, was found to possess virtues which neither the proponents nor the opponents of its original form anticipated. It became the symbol of the continuing will and unity of a nation as distinguished from the momentary will, embodied in specific governments. The power of parliament on the other hand became a more flexible expression of the national will than our more unwieldy system. In some European nations this flexibility is not matched by steadiness. But in the smaller north and west European nations, as well as in Britain, instruments of democratic society, developed out of the older feudal forms, lack no virtue possessed by the American system; and they exhibit some of the wisdom inherent in the more organic forms of society, which the more rationalistic conceptions of a purely bourgeois order lack.

In whatever way we estimate the relative merits and virtues of the European form of democracy in comparison with our own, it is evident that the original conception of a sharp distinction between a virtuous new democratic world and a vicious tyrannical older world was erroneous. The paths of progress in history have in this, as in many other instances, proved to be more devious and unpredictable than the putative managers of history could understand. The course of history refused to conform to the logic prescribed for it. The democratic dreamers were almost as wrong as the communist planners. They were right in so far as there was implicit in the democratic conception (though not always fully understood)

78

some modest awareness of the many sources of virtue, wisdom, and power in history and of the necessity to come to terms with them. The course of history cannot be coerced from a particular point in history and in accordance with a particular conception of its end.

Today the success of America in world politics depends upon its ability to establish community with many nations, despite the hazards created by pride of power on the one hand and the envy of the weak on the other. This success requires a modest awareness of the contingent elements in the values and ideals of our devotion, even when they appear to us to be universally valid; and a generous appreciation of the valid elements in the practices and institutions of other nations though they deviate from our own. In other words, our success in world politics necessitates a disavowal of the pretentious elements in our original dream, and a recognition of the values and virtues which enter into history in unpredictable ways and which defy the logic which either liberal or Marxist planners had conceived for it.

This American experience is a refutation in parable of the whole effort to bring the vast forces of history under the control of any particular will, informed by a particular ideal. All such efforts are rooted in what seems at first glance to be a contradictory combination of voluntarism and determinism. These efforts are on the one hand excessively voluntaristic, assigning a power to the human will and a purity to the mind of some men which no mortal or group of mortals possesses. On the other hand they are excessively deterministic since they regard most men as merely the creatures of an historical process.

Sometimes the historical process is conceived as a purely natural one, in which case all men are regarded as merely the instruments and fruits of the process. But generally it is assumed that some group of men has the intelligence to manipulate and manage the process. The excessive voluntarism which underlies this theory of an elite, explicit in communism and implicit in some democratic theory, is encouraged by the excessive determinism, which assumes that most men are creatures with simple determinate ends of life, and that their "anti-social" tendencies are quasi-biological impulses and inheritances which an astute social and psychological science can overcome or "redirect" to what are known as "socially approved" goals.

In a letter to the journal *Science* this naïve belief, widely held particularly in America, is succinctly expressed: "For if by employing the methods of science, men can come to understand and control the atom, there is reasonable likelihood that they can in the same way learn and control human group behaviour. . . . It is quite within reasonable probability that social science can provide the technics (for keeping the peace) if it is given a like amount of support afforded to the physical sciences in developing the atomic bomb."*

This belief which has found classic expression in the philosophy of John Dewey, pervades the academic disciplines of sociology and psychology.** Underlying this

*Quoted by Leslie A. White in *The Science of Culture*, p. 342.

**It would be absurd to claim any degree of unanimity in these disciplines, for frequently a debate rages between excessive determinists and excessive voluntarists. In the field of anthropology which has lately

THE MASTER OF DESTINY

whole view of history is the assumption that the realm
of history is only slightly distinguished from the realm
of nature. All the complexities arising in human history
from the fact that human agents, who are a part of the
process of history, are also its creators, are obscured. The
historical character of man as both agent in, and creature
of, history is not recognized.

---

entered the lists in the study and direction of contemporary culture, a
strong school of cultural determinists challenges the voluntarists. The
determinists rightly recognize that man is the creature of his culture
and fail to see that he is also the creator of it. Thus a cultural de-
terminist may rather amusingly challenge the excessive voluntarism of
a psychologist. Leslie White in *The Science of Culture* quotes Professor
Gordon Allport as observing: "The United States spent two billion dol-
lars in the invention of the atomic bomb, and asks 'What is there absurd
in spending an equivalent sum if necessary on the discovery of the
means of control?'" Obviously such reasoning assumes that the vast
and complex processes of action and interaction between human wills
and desires can be brought "under control" if only sufficient money is
spent on the enterprise.

Mr. White, who regards this view as "unsound," proceeds to challenge
it with an equally unsound view: "Wars are struggles between social
organisms, called nations," he declares, "for survival, struggles for the
possession and use of the resources of the earth, for fertile fields, coal,
oil, and iron deposits. . . . No amount of understanding will alter or
remove the basis of this struggle any more than an understanding of
the ocean's tides will diminish or terminate the flow" (Leslie A. White in
The Science of Culture, p. 343).

There is an absolute contradiction between these two theories in so
far as one assumes and the other denies that there can be an elite group
with minds pure enough to transcend the "struggle between social organisms" and powerful enough to compose the struggle.

But the theories have much in common, in each case the historical
process is regarded as similar in kind with the natural process. The
wars of history are regarded as perfectly analogous to "the ocean's
tides." What men think about the peril of an atomic bomb is regarded
as equally manageable with the physical forces which produce the bomb.

81

Man as an historical creature never has as pure and disinterested a mind and his "values" and "socially approved goals" are never as universally valid as the prospective managers and manipulators of historical destiny assume theirs to be. This is true of the communist oligarchs as tutors of a disinterested proletariat. They are blind not only to their own lust of power, but also to the partial and particular viewpoint of the disinherited, and the special interests of a Russian nation as well as to every other historical contingency which taints the purity of their position. But it is also true of an American nation, or any other nation with Messianic illusions. It is particularly true of the host of modern social, psychological or anthropological scientists, who think it an easy matter to match the disinterestedness of the natural scientist in the field of historical values. They all forget that, though man has a limited freedom over the historical process, he remains immersed in it. None of them deal profoundly with the complex "self" whether in its individual or in its collective form. This self has a reason; but its reason is more intimately related to the anxieties and fears, the hopes and ambitions of the self as spirit and to the immediate necessities of the self as natural organism than the "pure" reason of the natural scientist; for he observes forces of nature which do not essentially challenge the hopes and fears of the self.*

If one speaks of a "collective form" of selfhood, one

*In his address at the Convocation of the Massachusetts Institute of Technology, March 30, 1949, Mr. Winston Churchill declared: "The Dean of the humanities spoke with awe 'of an approaching scientific ability to control men's thoughts with precision.'—I shall be very content to be dead before that happens."

need not enter into the inconclusive debate whether human communities can be said to possess "personality." They obviously do not have a single organ of self-transcendence, though a political community has an inchoate organ of will in its government. Yet they do have the capacity to stand beyond themselves, observe and estimate their behavior, and trace the course of their history in terms of some framework of meaning which gives them a sense of continuing identity amidst the flux of time. These estimates are made not by a single mind but by competing "minds" and "schools" of thought, so that every nation or other community is involved in a continuous debate about what it is or ought to be. But even this debate, which sharply distinguishes the collective self from the more integral individual self, has analogies in individual life. For the individual is also involved in a perpetual internal dialogue about the legitimacy of his hopes and purposes, and the virtue or vice of his previous acts. In this dialogue contrition and complacency, pride of accomplishment and a sense of inadequacy, alternate in ways not too different from the alternation of moods in a community.

In any event, the significant unit of thought and action in the realm of historical encounter is not a mind but a self. This unit has an organic unity of rational, emotional and volitional elements which make all its actions and attitudes historically more relative than is realized in any moment of thought and action. The inevitability of this confusion between the relative and the universal is exactly what is meant by original sin. It is the rejection of the reality of original sin in the mind of the controllers of social process which has bred either cruelty or confusion. It has bred cruelty if the elite managed to achieve power proportioned to their pretensions and confusion if they only wistfully longed for it.

But if the mind or the will which pretends to control historical destiny is more "historical" than is realized in one sense of the word, the lives and persons, the forces and emotions, the hopes and fears which are to be managed and controlled are more "historical" in another sense of the word. For man as an historical creature has desires of indeterminate dimensions. Unique human freedom, in even the simplest peasant, transfigures nature's immediate necessities. This freedom imparts a stubborn recalcitrance to his actions which make him finally "unmanageable." It transmutes all of nature's necessities into indeterminate ambitions which traditional societies have actually held within bounds more successfully than modern societies. But they will always prevent that simple social harmony which is the utopia of both democratic and communist idealists. This unique freedom is the generator of both the destructiveness and the creativity of man. Most of the efforts to manage the historical process would actually destroy the creativity with the destructiveness.*

There are strong ironic aspects in the tremendous labors

*In a naïve psychologist's view of utopia, B. F. Skinner's *Walden II*, we are presented with the vision of an ideal community of six hundred souls who have been conditioned to a life of perfect harmony, free of all excessive ambition or jealousy. The psychologist who has created this community admits that he has "managed" the development of the individual components of the harmonious community and that there are, therefore, similarities between him and the notorious dictators of of our contemporary wise men to isolate the roots of human aggressiveness, to determine how frustration may be related to racial prejudice and to study the cause of "social tensions" everywhere. For all their labors are based upon the assumption that they are dealing primarily with measurable forms of insecurity or "antisocial" tendencies or "irrational" behavior which will yield to some special technique. Meanwhile the world is confronted by a mania which represents the corruption of a characteristically historic tendency in man. Communism is compounded of Messianism and a lust for power. The Messianism is a corrupt expression of man's search for the ultimate within the vicissitudes and hazards of time. The lust for power contains spiritual elements mixed with the natural survival impulse of the world of nature. Neither element in the compound can be measured either in the communist theories of human nature or in those of most "liberals" who are trying to save us from communism.

Elaborate theories are also evolved about the roots of human aggressiveness. The anthropologists have a particular penchant for discovering those roots in the early toilet training or in the methods of mothers for swaddling children.* The Germans, the Japanese and the Russians have all been analyzed in the hope of discovering the

---

*Geoffrey Gorer and John Rickman, *The People of Great Russia,* and an article by Ruth Benedict, "Child Rearing in Certain European Countries," in *American Journal of Orthopsychiatry,* 1949.

---

our day. But he feels that there is a great distinction between him and them because he has done what he has done for the good of the community. The community meanwhile lacks the heroïc and noble elements in human nature as completely as destructive animosities.

85

secret of their aggressive behavior in their traditions of child training. Significantly it has not been determined whether collective aggressiveness is merely the cumulation of individual forms of aggressiveness or whether it is the fruit of an undue docility among the individuals of a nation which provides fodder for the aggressiveness of its leaders.

A very noted psychiatrist, head of the World Health Organization, thinks that human aggressiveness is derived from the fact that "we are civilized too early" which is to say that we are prompted to regard our "natural human urges as bad." Thus we "distrust and hate ourselves" and from this self-hatred arises "aggressive feelings against others." This aggressiveness could be cured very easily if mothers' clinics were established which would teach mothers that "babies need, not just want but need, uncritical love, love whose manifestations are quite independent of the babies' behaviour." Such love will create the feeling of "belonging" which in a "successful development process should spread gradually to include family, friends and fellow citizens and in the little world this has become it can no longer safely stop at national boundaries." We must now have "large numbers of people who have grown emotionally beyond national boundaries" and we, therefore, need a greater emphasis on "uncritical love" and "freedom from the 'conviction of sin.' "*

It is not explained how both liberal and Marxist civilizations which have long since disavowed doctrines

*Brock Chisholm in an article, "Social Responsibility," in *Science,* Jan. 14, 1949.

which Dr. Chisholm abhors should have generated so much "aggresiveness".

A survey of much of the current literature of our modern wise men must impress the reader with the ironic deterioration of wisdom, consequent upon this pretension of wisdom. Everything that is really historical in both the true aspirations and the monstrous ambitions of men is obscured. And these animadversions are carried on while we face a threat arising from depths in the human soul which are not subject to these measurements, and from aberrations which are strikingly similar to those of our deliverers.

Sometimes our modern wise men move illogically from the real world of history to the dream world of "natural instincts." Thus Bertrand Russell, who has disavowed his earlier pacifism and has recently counseled America not to be too squeamish in using our atomic weapons against the Russians, sometimes thinks in another frame of meaning in which all our military expenditures are seen as "due to impulses incorporated into human nature by long ages of training and natural selection."*

*Bertrand Russell in an article, "The Modern Mastery of Nature," *Listener* (London), May, 1951. "What a nation can spare from increasing its own numbers," declares Mr. Russell, "it devotes only in part to its own welfare. To a very great extent it devotes its energies to killing other people. . . . The United States government has announced that in the coming year 20% of its total production is to be spent on armaments." Mr. Russell's facts are indisputable. But the idea that the American people bear this tremendous burden because they are blinded by "impulses incorporated into human nature by long ages of training and natural selection" is rather naïve, particularly in the light of Mr. Russell's belief that we must be armed against communism and must not even be too squeamish about the bomb.

Perhaps the real difficulty in both the communist and the liberal dreams of a "rationally ordered" historic process is that the modern man lacks the humility to accept the fact that the whole drama of history is enacted in a frame of meaning too large for human comprehension or management. It is a drama in which fragmentary meanings can be discerned within a penumbra of mystery; and in which specific duties and responsibilities can be undertaken within a vast web of relations which are beyond our powers.

A sane life requires that we have some clues to the mystery so that the realm of meaning is not simply reduced to the comprehensible processes of nature. But these clues are ascertained by faith, which modern man has lost. So he hovers ambivalently between subjection to the "reason" which he can find in nature and the "reason" which he can impose upon nature. But neither form of reason is adequate for the comprehension of the illogical and contradictory patterns of the historic drama, and for anticipating the emergence of unpredictable virtues and vices. In either case, man as the spectator and manager of history imagines himself to be freer of the drama he beholds than he really is; and man as the creature of history is too simply reduced to the status of a creature of nature, and all of his contacts to the ultimate are destroyed.

CHAPTER V

The Triumph of Experience
Over Dogma

1

IF the experiences of America as a world power, its responsibilities and concomitant guilt, its frustrations and its discovery of the limits of power, constitute an ironic refutation of some of the most cherished illusions of a liberal age, its experiences in domestic politics represent an ironic form of success. Our success in establishing justice and insuring domestic tranquillity has exceeded the characteristic insights of a bourgeois culture. Frequently our success is due to social and political policies which violate and defy the social creed which characterizes a commercial society. America has developed a pragmatic approach to political and economic questions which would do credit to Edmund Burke, the great exponent of the wisdom of historical experience as opposed to the abstract rationalism of the French Revolution.

Marxism is engaged in two types of contest with the bourgeois world. In the one it has become the fighting creed of the peoples of decaying agrarian civilizations in conflict with the democratic-industrial world. In the other, parliamentary forms of Marxism inform the political parties of industrial workers in industrial nations as these challenge the economic and political power of capital and industry. In the international contest between Marxism and the democratic world, it is ideologically unfortunate that the most powerful nation in the alliance of free nations should also be most consistently bourgeois in its attitudes. This gives the communist propaganda some undue advantages as may be seen in the prejudices of the Asian world against our alleged capitalistic imperialism. In terms of their ancient resentments and of their newfound communist creed, we are, by definition, "imperialistic," and our very success and power seem to give plausibility to the indictment.

But in the contest betwen Marxism and bourgeois ideology within the confines of western civilization and in the domestic politics of its several nations we play a different role. We may be the most consistent bourgeois nation; but we have established a degree of justice which has prevented the Marxist movement from arising in our society in either its milder or more virulent form. This achievement may be due primarily to our highly favored circumstances. For the wealth of our natural resources, the unity of a continental economy and the efficiency of our technology have, as we have previously noted, mitigated the severity of the social struggle in America.

But there are other reasons for this achievement. The contest between Marxism and the bourgeois world is a debate between two ideologies, each of which proceeds confidently to certain conclusions upon the basis of presuppositions which are only partly true. Marxism is so formidable as a political creed precisely because it expresses the convictions of those who have discovered the errors in the liberal-bourgeois creed in bitter experience. Marxism is so dangerous because in its consistent form it usually substitutes a more grievous error for the error which it challenges. In this debate between errors, or between half-truth and half-truth, America is usually completely on the side of the bourgeois credo in theory; but in practice it has achieved balances of power in the organization of social forces and a consequent justice which has robbed the Marxist challenge of its sting. No one sings odes to liberty as the final end of life with greater fervor than Americans. But in practice we heed the warning of Edmund Burke: "I should therefore suspend my congratulations on the new liberty of France until I am informed how it has been combined with government, with public force, with the disciplines and obedience of armies; with the collection of effective and well-distributed revenue; with morality and religion; with the solidity of property; with peace and order. . . . *Liberty, when men act in bodies, is power.* Considerate people, before they declare themselves, will observe the use which is made of power."*

Britain has been, until recently, the home of pragmatic politics, where "liberty broadened down from precedent to precedent"; where the complex relation of freedom to order was so well understood that social policy moved from case to case and point to point, informed by experience rather than consistent dogma; and thereby avoiding a too great sacrifice of freedom to order or of

*Edmund Burke, *Reflections on the French Revolution*, Chapter I.

order to freedom. Britain has not lost its genius for the empirical approach; but we may have exceeded her achievements in some respects, partly because we had margins of security which prevented the rise of consistent dogmas. Our favored position may tempt us to reject whatever truth is embodied in the Marxist creed too unreservedly; but British labor has become increasingly inclined to meet disillusionments merely by a more consistent application of its creed.

2

A consideration of some of the crucial issues in the debate between Marxism and a liberal society may illumine the paradox of American social policy, whose theory is usually consistently on the one side of the debate while its practice frequently strikes a creative synthesis. A bourgeois society regards the achievement of social harmony as fairly easy. It tends to believe that it is only necessary to remove irrelevant political restraints from economic activity; and then the "natural system of liberty" will become effective. It believes that the self-interest of each individual is checked and balanced by that of every other individual. If this check is not sufficient, an "enlightened" self-interest which knows how to find the point of concurrence between the interests of self and those of the community will ostensibly supply the deficiency. This serene confidence in the possibilities of social harmony is derived both from one of the great achievements of a commercial culture, and from a natural illusion of such a culture. The achievement was the discovery that men could be brought most effectively into the vast system of mutual services in a complex society by engaging their "self-interest" rather than their "benevolence." The cobbler would make shoes and the farmer would raise wheat and the tailor would fashion a coat; and they would exchange their several products. Each would gain in the exchange; for it permitted a specialization of labor which improved the efficiency of each. Each would seek his own gain, or rather that of his family; but each would be prompted to serve the other in the system. There are elements of truth in this discovery of classical economics which remain a permanent treasure of a free society, since some forms of a "free market" are essential to democracy. The alternative is the regulation of economic process through bureaucratic-political decisions. Such regulation, too consistently applied, involves the final peril of combining political and economic power.

On the other hand, the liberal society never achieved the perfect harmony of which it dreamed because it overestimated the reciprocity of the free market and also equated economic competition with all encounters in society. It overestimated the reciprocity of the market because it was oblivious both to the elements of power in society, and to the disproportions of power in economic life. Power, in the thought of the typically bourgeois man, is political. He believes that it must be reduced to a minimum. The earlier bourgeois man wanted to eliminate political power because it represented the special advantages which the old aristocracy had over him. The present bourgeois man wants to reduce it to a minimum because it represents the effort of a democratic society to bring disproportions of economic power under control. In the shift of motive from earlier to later bourgeois man lies the inevitable degradation of the liberal dogma. Marxism was bound to challenge the dogma, and to find the later form particularly vulnerable.

The reciprocity of the market was too simply equated with the social harmony of the community because self-interest was restricted to the economic motive. The false abstraction of "economic man" remains a permanent defect in all bourgeois-liberal ideology. It seems to know nothing of what Thomas Hobbes termed "the continual competition for honor and dignity" in human affairs. It understands neither the traditional ethnic and cultural loyalties which qualify a consistent economic rationalism; nor the deep and complex motives in the human psyche which express themselves in the desire for "power and glory." All the conflicts in human society involving passions and ambitions, hatreds and loves, envies and ideals not recorded in the market place, are beyond the comprehension of the typical bourgeois ethos.

Inevitably this meant that social realities would develop which were not anticipated in the creed. The strong would and did take advantage of the weak. Prudence was not wise or strong enough to deter them. The earlier industrialism did aggravate, rather than mitigate, the lot of the poor, as certainly as it accentuated the disproportions of power existing in traditional societies. Reason which, according to the liberal creed, would always seek the point of concurrence between the interests of the self and of the other, could not function consistently in this manner. Rather it conformed to Thomas Hobbes' conception of the function of reason. It would make demands upon the community which seemed reasonable to the claimant and inordinate from the standpoint of the community. In these social realities the Marxist challenge arose. In place of the picture of an actual or potential social harmony in bourgeois society it put the idea of a class conflict, running through the whole of human history and reaching its climax in the very society which, in its own esteem, had created a potential social harmony by its system of "natural liberty." More conscious of the power element in life than liberalism, Marxism made an even greater error than liberalism in identifying the locus of power. In Marxist thought political power is always subordinate to, and the tool of, economic power. Government is always bogus. It is never more than the executive committee of the propertied classes. This is an even more grievous mistake than the liberal error of obscuring the reality of economic power. Marxism added another mistake to this error. It ascribed economic power purely to ownership, thus hiding the power of the manager and manipulator. The consequence of these errors makes it possible for consistent Marxism to create an oligarchy in which the economic and political power in a community are combined while no checks are placed upon such inordinate concentration. According to the theory, the checks are not necessary since no one owns property; and ownership is the only source, both of the power and of the self-interest which prompts power to defy the welfare of the community.

The course of history has amply proved the miscalculations of the Marxist alternatives to a liberal society to

95

be even more grievously in error than the liberal ones. Nevertheless, it is not possible to establish justice amidst the vast concentration and competition of power in modern technical society if the illusions and miscalculations of a liberal society are not radically qualified.

This qualification has actually taken place in the political practice of America even though its political theory tends to conform to the general liberal creed. The early American culture was not bereft of a realistic theory. We have previously observed the two strains of thought, Calvinist and Jeffersonian, which entered into our original American heritage. On the problem of the resolution of potential conflicts of interest and power in the community, the strain of thought most perfectly expressed by James Madison combined Christian realism in the interpretation of human motives and desires with Jefferson's passion for liberty. The fellow Virginians, Madison and Jefferson, were prevented by their common passion for liberty from seriously debating this issue between them. The difference in the philosophies are, therefore, more frequently illumined by the exchange of letters between Adams and Jefferson than between Madison and Jefferson. Yet the difference is symbolized in the distinction between the presuppositions of the Declaration of Independence and of the Constitution of the United States, of which Jefferson and Madison are the respective inspirers.

Jefferson, and his coterie including Tom Paine, had a vision of an harmonious society in which government would interfere as little as possible with the economic ambitions of the individual. These ambitions were presumed to be moderate; and their satisfaction without friction with the neighbor would be guaranteed by the wide opportunities of the new continent. The subordination of man to man would be prevented by the simple expedient of preferring agriculture to industry. Jefferson's ideal society conformed perfectly to John Locke's conception of men "mixing their labor" with nature, and claiming the fruits thereof as their legitimate property.

Madison feared the potential tyranny of government as much as Jefferson; but he understood the necessity of government much more. The Constitution protects the citizen against abuses of government, not so much by keeping government weak as by introducing the principle of balance of power into government. This idea may have been derived from Calvin's suggestions in his *Institutes** by way of the teachings of John Witherspoon, Madison's teacher at Princeton (then the College of New Jersey). Whether this balance of power between executive, legislative and judicial functions is actually the best method of preventing the abuse of power is a question which is not relevant in this context. European democracies have found other methods of achieving the same end; and their methods may be less likely to issue in a mutual frustration of a community's governing powers. The important fact is that the necessity of a strong government was recognized. Madison was much more conscious than Jef-

*Calvin's words are: "The vice or imperfection of men therefore renders it safer and more tolerable for government to be in the hands of many, that they may afford each other mutual admonition and assistance and that if any one arrogate to himself more than his right, the many may act as censors and masters to restrain his ambition." *Institutes*, IV, 20, 8.

ferson of the peril of what he called "faction" in the community. He had no hope of resolving such conflicts by simple prudence. With the realists of every age he knew how intimately man's reason is related to his interests. "As long as any connection exists," he wrote, "between man's reason and his self-love, his opinions and passions will have reciprocal influence upon each other."* He even anticipated Marx in finding disproportions in the possession of property to be the primary cause of political and social friction: "The most common and durable source of faction," he declared, "has been the various and unequal distribution of property." He regarded this inequality as the inevitable consequence of unequal abilities among citizens. One of Madison's most persuasive arguments for a federal union was his belief that a community of wide expanse would so diffuse interests and passions as to prevent the turbulent form of political strife, to which he regarded small communities subject. The development of parties in America has partly refuted the belief that interests could not be nationally organized. Yet the interests which are organized in the two great parties of America are so diverse as to prevent the parties from being unambiguous ideological instruments. Thus, history has partly justified his conviction.

In any event the political philosophy which underlies our Constitution is characterized by a shrewd awareness of the potential conflicts of power and passion in every community. It knows nothing of a simple harmony in society, analogous to the alleged reciprocity of the free market.

*Federalist Papers, No. 10.

Our political experience has enlarged upon this wisdom without always being in conscious relation to its explicit early formulation. The American labor movement was almost completely bereft of the ideological weapons, which the rebellious industrial masses of Europe carried. In its inception it disavowed not only Marxist revolutionary formulas but every kind of political program. It was a pragmatic movement, born of the necessity of setting organized power against organized power in a technical society. Gradually it became conscious of the fact that economic power does try to bend government to its own ends. It has, therefore, decided to challenge a combination of political and economic power with a like combination of its own. These developments have been very recent; but they have also been very rapid.

Naturally, the "semi-official" creed of a bourgeois community, as distinguished from the philosophy which informs our Constitution, was arrayed against this development. The right of collective bargaining was declared to be a violation of the rights of employers to hire or fire whom they would. Supreme Court decisions, directed against the labor movement, were informed by the generally accepted individualistic creed.* But ultimately, in the words of "Mr. Dooley," the court decisions "followed the election returns." Long before the "New Deal" radically changed the climate of American political life the

*At the turn of the century a Supreme Court decision declared that, "It is the constitutional right of the employer to dispense with the services of an employee because of his membership in a labor union." In another decision the Court declared, "To ask a man to agree in advance to refrain from affiliation with a union—is not to ask him to give up any part of his constitutional freedom."

99

sovereign power of government had been used to enforce taxation laws which embodied social policy as well as revenue necessities; great concentrations of power in industry were broken up by law; necessary monopolies in utilities were brought under political regulation; social welfare, security and health and other values which proved to be outside the operations of the free market were secured by political policy. More recently, housing, medicine and social security have become matters of public and political policy. All this has been accomplished on a purely pragmatic basis, without the ideological baggage which European labor carried.

The development of American democracy toward a welfare state has proceeded so rapidly partly because the ideological struggle was not unnecessarily sharpened. It has proceeded so rapidly in fact that the question must be raised in America, as well as in the more collectivist states of Europe, whether the scope of bureaucratic decisions may not become too wide and the room for the automatic balances of unregulated choices too narrow.

These are misgivings which will confront every modern democracy and may confront them till doomsday, since there is no neat principle which will solve the relation of power to justice and of justice to freedom. The significant point in the American development is that here, no less than in Europe, a democratic political community has had enough virtue and honesty to disprove the Marxist indictment that government is merely the instrument of privileged classes. It has established sufficient justice to prevent the outbreak of the social resentments which have wrecked the less healthy European nations and have created social acerbities exceeding our own in the best of them.

We have, in short, achieved such justice as we possess in the only way justice can be achieved in a technical society: we have equilibrated power. We have attained a certain equilibrium in economic society itself by setting organized power against organized power. When that did not suffice we used the more broadly based political power to redress disproportions and disbalances in economic society.

3

What has become of our social peace in this contest of power? The acrimonies of party strife are considerable among us. The absence of collectivist or revolutionary ideology among the workers does not save them from charges of being revolutionaries. Yet the business community accepts the general development of democracy in America with a certain degree of practical grace even while it wars against it ideologically. This is why we are so completely misunderstood in Europe. For Europe knows our semi-official ideology better than it knows our practical justice.

It knows that our business men talk endlessly of liberty in accents which Europeans, particularly Continentals, associate with a decayed liberalism, transmuted into a vexatious conservatism. But Europe seems not to know that our business men sign five-year contracts with labor unions, containing "escalator clauses" guaranteeing rising wages with rising prices. American business in practice has in short accepted the power of labor; it has even incorporated the idea of the necessity of high wages as a basis for mass production into its social philosophy. It acknowledges the "right of collective bargaining" in the various creeds of liberty by which it seeks to popularize the "American way of life."

Some of our social peace must be accredited to the fluid class structure of American society. This has influenced the ethos of both worker and business man. The Marxist class concept, designed for a class in industrial society, has taken deep root only where a previous feudal class structure has reinforced the social resentments created by industrial injustice. The American business community has frequently made the silly charge that Marxists invented the class conflict or even the class structure. The charge is the more absurd since it is quite probable that the American class structure will become more fixed as the nation moves toward the final limits of an expanding economy. It is true, nevertheless, that Marxism obscures the complexity of the class structure in an industrial society as certainly as the liberal creed obscures the realities of class tensions. But if the dynamics of an industrial society are superimposed upon the class distinctions of a feudal order, the psychological facts correspond much more closely to the Marxist picture of class antagonisms than they do in a purer bourgeois community such as our own. This is certainly one reason why Britain, in many respects a more integral community than ours and boasting of democratic achievements comparable with, or exceeding, our own, was bound to create a political party more heavily loaded with Marxist ideology than ours. The very achievements of British political democracy, through which it was possible to move from a feudal to a commercial and from a commercial to an industrial society without a serious rent in the social or cultural fabric, has the one serious disadvantage of preserving a residual feudal class snobbishness, which even an era of socialist politics has not eradicated.

The fluidity of the American class structure is primarily a gift of providence, being the consequence of a constantly expanding economy. But this good fortune has been transmuted into social virtue insofar as it has not only left the worker comparatively free of social resentments but also tends to make the privileged classes less intransigent in their resistance to the rising classes. "The absence of significant social resentments in American life," declared a recent Continental visitor, "has left a deeper impression upon me than any other American characteristic." The higher British classes may yield more gracefully than ours in the political struggle; but they retain the weapon of social contempt to compensate for their loss of political and economic power.

4

The achievement of America in developing social policies which are wiser than its social creed and closer to the truth than either Marxist or bourgeois ideology is subject to two important reservations. First, the debate in the western world on the institution of property was aborted in America. Nothing in the conflicting ideologies of Marxism and the bourgeois culture reveals the contrast between them so much as their respective attitudes toward property. Property is the instrument of justice in the creed of the bourgeois world; and the source of all evil in the Marxist interpretation. Both creeds miss the truth about property. Since property is a form of power, it cannot be unambiguously a source of social peace and justice. For every form of power, when inordinate or irresponsible, can be a tool of aggression and injustice. However, since property is not the only type of power in society (not even of all economic power), it cannot be the sole source of injustice. Since some forms of property represent the security of the home, and others protect against the hazards of the future and still others are instruments for the proper performance of our social function, some forms of property are obviously instruments of social justice and peace.

Clearly the Marxist and the bourgeois property ideologies are equally indiscriminate. The Marxist ideology has proved to be the more dangerous because, under the cover of its illusions, a new society has been created in which political and economic power are monstrously combined while the illusion is fostered that economic power has been completely eliminated through the "socialization" of property. A democratic society on the other hand preserves a modicum of justice by various strategies of distributing and balancing both economic and political power. But it is not tenable to place the institution of property into the realm of the sacrosanct. Every human institution must stand under constant review. The question must be asked, what forms of it are viable under what specific conditions? In so far as the absence of a Marxist challenge to our culture has left the institution of property completely unchallenged we may have become the prisoners of a dogmatism which will cost us dearly in some future crisis.

The second weakness in the American political and economic situation is that the lip service which the whole culture pays to the principles of *laissez-faire* makes for tardiness in dealing with the instability of a free economy, when the perils of inflation or deflation arise. They are finally dealt with pragmatically; but not before the consequences of inaction have become very apparent. Some believe that the lessons taught in the great depression of 1929 have been so well learned that a recurrence of such a catastrophe is impossible; but it is not altogether certain that this is true. It is certainly true that the semi-official ideology of the culture prevents adequate measures from being taken in time against the perils of inflation in periods of war production, such as the present one. Thus, the American business community is inclined to speak of our economy in terms of lyrical praise which suggest that we have solved the ultimate problems of both justice and stability. But the individual members of the community speculate anxiously and endlessly over the immediate prospects of one or other of the twin evils of deflation and inflation. From the viewpoint of Europe, whose economic health has become so dependent on the American giant that a tremor in our system creates serious shocks in the world economy, we remain an irritatingly incalculable element in world stability.

With these reservations we may claim that the unarticulated wisdom embodied in the actual experience of American life has created forms of justice considerably higher than our more articulate unwisdom suggests.

5

Any modern community which establishes a tolerable justice is the beneficiary of the ironic triumph of the wisdom of common sense over the foolishness of its wise men. For the wise men are inevitably tempted to follow either one or the other line of "rational" advance of which the bourgeois and the Marxist ideologies are perfect types. The one form of thought regards all social and historical processes as self-regulating. In this case it is only required to eliminate the foolish restraints and controls which former generations have sought to place upon them. This is, on the whole, the conception of rational politics and economics of the bourgeois era since the French Enlightenment. The alternative type of thought conceives a social or historical goal, presumably desired by all humanity, and seeks to "plan" for its achievement.

The debate between those who want to plan and those who want to remove as many restraints as possible from human activities transcends the limits of the political controversy between the industrial workers and the middle class by which it is best known in modern life. But that controversy offers a perfect illustration of the "ideological taint" which colors the reason of each type of thought. Middle-class life came to power and wealth by breaking ancient restraints; and the more successful middle classes fear new restraints upon their sometimes quite inordinate powers and privileges. They, therefore, speak piously and reverently of "the laws of nature" which must not be violated; and they endow the unpredictable drama of human history with fixities of nature not to be found there.

The industrial classes, on the other hand, found themselves in an unfavorable situation in this celebrated "free" world. They were involved in a vast social mechanism which periodically broke down; and they were not consoled by the belief that these crises were necessary for society's health. They lacked the personal skills to enter on even terms in an individualistic competitive struggle; and they were confronted in any case with consolidations of power which they could not match. In fairly honest democracies they saw the possibility of organizing both economic and political power to match that of the more privileged classes. In the less healthy democracies or undemocratic nations, their fears and resentments found assuagement in the Marxist scheme which envisaged not only a "plan" of justice for society but of redemption for the whole of mankind. But these political programs, even when they are only mildly Marxist, are also bound to have their ideological weakness. They are more or less oblivious to the many forms of initiative in society which even the wisest plan may destroy; and they are unconscious of the peril of combining political and economic power which inheres in every plan.

The triumph of the wisdom of common sense over these two types of wisdom is, therefore, primarily the wisdom of democracy itself, which prevents either strategy from being carried through to its logical conclusion. There is an element of truth in each position which becomes falsehood, precisely when it is carried through too consistently. The element of truth in each creed is required to do full justice to man's real situation. For man transcends the social and historical process sufficiently to make it possible

107

and necessary deliberately to contrive common ends of life, particularly the end of justice. He cannot count on inadvertence and the coincidence of private desires alone to achieve common ends. On the other hand, man is too immersed in the welter of interest and passion in history and his survey over the total process is too short-range and limited to justify the endowment of any group or institution of "planners" with complete power. The "purity" of their idealism and the pretensions of their science must always be suspect. Man simply does not have a "pure" reason in human affairs; and if such reason as he has is given complete power to attain its ends, the taint will become the more noxious.

The controversy between those who would "plan" justice and order and those who trust in freedom to establish both is, therefore, an irresolvable one. Every healthy society will live in the tension of that controversy until the end of history; and will prove its health by preventing either side from gaining complete victory.

The triumph of "common sense" in American history is thus primarily the triumph of the vitality of our democratic institutions. The ironic feature in it consists of the fact that we have achieved a tolerable synthesis between two conflicting ideologies in practice while we allowed the one to dominate our theory.

CHAPTER VI

The International
Class Struggle

1

THE hegemonic position of the United States in the community of nations would have been morally precarious, even if an international class war had not intervened to aggravate the difficulties. It is not easy, as we have seen, for an adolescent nation, with illusions of childlike innocency to come to terms with the responsibilities and hazards of global politics in an atomic age.

But all these perplexities have been heightened by the fact that a class war, originally designed for industrial society and aborted there, has become the dominant pattern of international relations. This development is partly due to the fact that Russia is at once a great center of power and the holy land of a world-wide revolutionary religion. But this fact alone would not have created the hazardous situation which confronts us, if this revolutionary religion had not taken root among the poor peoples of non-industrial nations, particularly in Asia, and if the portents were not so favorable for its continued expansion there. The fact is that an ideology designed for what Toynbee defined as the "internal proletariat" has been able to recoup its defeats in the healthy industrial nations by becoming a remarkably "live option" for the "external proletariat," the poverty-stricken peoples of traditional agrarian economics.

In this situation the hegemony of America in the community of the free world creates some curious moral hazards. We are ironically held responsible for disparities in wealth and well-being which are chiefly due to differences in standards of productivity. But they lend themselves with a remarkable degree of plausibility to the Marxist indictment, which attributes all such differences to exploitation. Thus, every effort we make to prove the virtue of our "way of life" by calling attention to our prosperity is used by our enemies and detractors as proof of our guilt. Our experience of an ironic guilt when we pretend to be innocent is thus balanced by the irony of an alleged guilt when we are comparatively innocent. We find these charges against us difficult to understand because we are the most consistently bourgeois nation on earth. We are, therefore, not fully conversant with the ethos in which the resentments of communism are generated.

While the dynamism of industrial civilization at first heightened the feudal inequalities of privilege, it ultimately introduced complexities and fluidities into the class structure which alleviated the hopelessness and desperation of the poor. Thus it tended to make the orthodox Marxist interpretation of their lot implausible and irrelevant. Marxism has been most successful in those

110

industrial nations of the West in which the realities of industrial society did not efface the older feudal class structure. It has been least successful among us, who had no feudal past; or destroyed the remnant we had in our civil war. Significantly, the only western European nations in which communism is now a living creed, Italy and France, are those in which the historical dynamism of modern industrialism has never shattered the traditional feudal ethos. In France, where feudalism was ostensibly broken by the classic bourgeois revolution, the bourgeoisie adopted the restrictive and undynamic social attitudes of the older feudalism and created a society in which the middle classes make no great efforts to increase productivity and fight desperately to prevent the working classes from gaining a larger share of productive wealth.

Since Marxism interprets political institutions in purely cynical terms, regarding all government as merely the "executive committee" of the privileged classes, therefore wherever democratic government has the power and the will to regulate economic forces for the sake of the general welfare, a good part of the Marxist indictment becomes otiose.

If those European nations, in which feudal and capitalistic injustices are compounded, are most receptive to the communist seeds, it cannot be surprising that the communist creed has become an even more attractive option for the desperate peoples of impoverished agrarian-feudal economies in the whole non-industrial world. It has thus become the standard of revolt of the non-industrial against the industrial world, though such a revolt

111

was originally considered possible only after capitalism had raised the injustices of the feudal world to such a pitch that the final climactic struggle between good and evil in history could take place. That this religious apocalypse, designed for industrial society, should be regarded as relevant for a non-industrial society, is partly the achievement of Lenin. He reinterpreted the sacred texts of Marxism to achieve this result. Through his shrewdness the Marxist revolution gained its first success in the semi-Asiatic, and almost wholly agrarian, culture of Russia. It is spreading from there into Asia and into the whole non-industrial world.

But no degree of reinterpretation of texts could have accomplished this result if the social and cultural forces in the non-industrial world had not been propitious. It is, therefore, necessary to enumerate and define some of these forces and factors.

The primary cause of the resentments which generate revolt in the non-industrial world is the fact that the first impact of a technical society upon a non-technical one was exploitative. The resentments created by this impact of "imperialism" and "colonialism" remain operative, even in a period in which the fading strength of the colonial powers has led to the emancipation of millions upon millions of former colonial peoples. The economic consequences of imperialism were certainly not as unambiguously evil as the Marxist propaganda claims; for it introduced technical skills and education to the agrarian world. Perhaps the most deleterious consequences of imperialism are in the spiritual rather than the economic realm. For arrogance is the inevitable consequence of the relation of power to weakness. In this case the arrogance of power reinforced ethnic prejudices; for the industrial world was "white" and the non-technical world was "colored."

Ironically our own nation, which has become the residuary legatee of these resentments, was not in the forefront of the imperial venture. Our economic base was so vast and self-sufficient as to obviate significant imperial ventures. Our economic power produced a great deal of covert imperialism. But we did not seek to govern other peoples politically. This fact makes some of the communist propaganda against us singularly irrelevant, as, for instance, the charge of the Chinese foreign minister that we are fighting in Korea in order to gain control of "markets" there for our capitalists.

Imperialism is a perennial problem of human existence; for powerful nations and individuals inevitably tend to use the weak as instruments of their purposes. If the ambitions of the powerful are not purely exploitative, as they frequently are not, they are nevertheless never as purely paternal as they pretend. The Marxist theory, by identifying this imperialist tendency with the capitalist system, enables a new type of imperialism to relate itself to the weakness of the non-industrial world, under the cover of an ostensibly pure benevolence. In theory Russian politics are the expression of solidarity between the sacred center of a political religion and its various mission fields. Thus the Marxist channeling of the resentments of the recently emancipated, or not yet fully emancipated, colonial peoples not only accentuates the primary animus of their rebellion but also, ironically, predisposes them to court enslavement to a new master, under the illusion that he is an emancipator.

The second reason for the rebellion of the non-industrial world is the plight of the poor in the non-technical world. This poverty has hardly been alleviated by political emancipation. Sometimes it has been aggravated by the social and political confusion consequent upon emancipation. This poverty has two sources: (a) feudal injustice and (b) the low productivity of agrarian economies. These economies have in many instances not reached the level of efficiency which European economies enjoyed before the Industrial Revolution.

All recently emancipated nations suffer from more grievous economic ills than the evils of political tutelage from which they revolted. Landlordism and usurious interest rates have been the engines of injustices in traditional cultures since the earliest agrarian civilizations of Egypt and Babylon. While China, the one traditional nation with a large number of freeholds, suffered less from landlordism, the corruptions of a vast bureaucracy produced analogous injustices. It is not at all certain that India, despite its democratic constitution and the idealism of its leaders, will be able to overcome the injustices of its feudal order in time to stave off a powerful communist movement. Certainly the communist revolution in China gained its success because the previous regime could not establish tolerable justice or order. The whole Middle East is, moreover, in serious plight. For there a decadent Mohammedan feudal order is visibly disintegrating. The relation of western capitalism to these traditional feudal systems of the agrarian world is, of course, not guiltless. Sometimes, as in Indo-China, strategic necessities in our conflict with communism forced us into alliance with a discredited French colonialism. In other cases, however, as in Indonesia, we may well have acted more precipitately in favor of independence than was wise. In any case, the whole of the West, and more particularly the American hegemonic power, is held responsible for the post-imperial ills of the nontechnical cultures far beyond our deserts. One of the real spiritual evils of imperialism is that it obsesses a nation held in tutelage with the idea that all of its ills flow from the imperial occupation. This is never the case, particularly not if the colonial nation is deficient in capacities for self-government so that political confusion and economic chaos follow upon emancipation. But frustrated hopes combine easily with communist propaganda to hold the western nations as responsible for the ills which follow upon emancipation as for those which preceded it.

Moreover, few of the non-industrial nations have sufficiently high standards of honesty to make democratic government viable. Corruption in their bureaucracies may be a more potent source of injustice than the economic system. Their low standards of honesty may have many roots. One of them certainly is that the great traditional cultures of the Orient never inculcated an individual sense of responsibility to the larger community. They combined very refined cultures with very low forms of social integration, the village and the family remaining the only communities of significant loyalty. Dishonesty in the Orient, therefore, usually means that any action advantageous to the agent's family is morally justified. The resulting corruption of government seems to make the Marxist cynical interpretation of politics remarkably relevant.

However, even the most grievous injustices of the feudal world are not as responsible for the abject poverty of its agrarian poor as the low efficiency of its economy. Moreover, when industry is introduced, its first effect is, as it was in Occidental nations, to heighten the injustices. Liberal opinion in the western world rightly stresses the necessity for technical assistance in raising the productivity of the whole non-industrial world. But it usually does not recognize that, even if every form of exploitation is avoided in this development, it is not possible to transmute an agrarian culture into a technical civilization without vast cultural and social dislocations. To counter the force of communism in the agrarian world we are under the necessity of telescoping developments which required four centuries in European history.

Meanwhile the difference between our wealth and the poverty of the technically undeveloped world is interpreted by communist propaganda as irrefutable evidence of the exploitative character of our economy. We sometimes naïvely contribute to the effectiveness of this propaganda by unduly stressing the height of our standard of living as proof of our social virtues. Our propaganda is all the more ineffective because the standards of living of a highly industrialized nation are so improbable to the imagination of impoverished peasants of the Orient, that they cannot impress their social and political attitudes.*

*Even non-communist socialism is capable of regarding differences in standards of productivity as *prima facie* evidence of exploitation. In

The net effect of all these aberrations is that the hegemonic power of the non-communist world becomes the symbol of every past and present injustice. It is held responsible for every ill inhering in the whole historic situation. The indictment against us achieves the greater plausibility because the facts are interpreted through a Marxist ideology. According to this ideology, poverty is caused solely by exploitation. Such an explanation is no more true than the contrasting bourgeois belief that distinctions of poverty and wealth are due primarily to differences of skill, thrift and industry. The truth about poverty and wealth is not fully disclosed by either theory. But the Marxist theory has the advantage of satisfying a deep instinct in the human heart. It places the blame for an unfortunate situation entirely upon others.

Applied to the social realities of a particular national economy it actually comes nearer to the truth, but achieves less political relevance, than when applied to distinctions of poverty and wealth between nations. A national community is sufficiently integral to achieve fairly equal standards of productive efficiency and also to work toward the equalization of unequal privileges by various political strategies. Great disparities of wealth and poverty in a national community, therefore, rightly arouse moral resentment. But since this moral resentment can be effectively channeled into political action in healthy modern societies, the Marxist indictment loses its force in them. But differences in the living standards

the recent propaganda pamphlet of the Bevanites of the British Labor Party, "One Way Only," these differences are presented as convincing proof of nefarious elements in our politics.

of various nations are due primarily to disparities in natural resources and in productive efficiency. The disparities in technical efficiency have profound historical roots which cannot be overcome in a decade or even a century. The Marxist interpretation of inequalities between nations is, therefore, more untrue than its interpretation of such inequalities within a particular nation. But since the inequalities between highly industrialized nations and low-grade agrarian economies are greater than those within any particular nation, the Marxist theory is politically more appealing, though less true, when applied internationally. Thus Marxist political illusions have achieved a higher degree of plausibility in the "class struggle" between nations than they achieved in domestic politics. Therefore we confront the ironic situation in world politics that the most powerful and technically the most efficient modern nation is condemned in a court of public opinion, strongly influenced by Marxist dogma, not so much for its real sins as for achievements in which it takes an inordinate pride. This is one of many reasons why we must not expect to gain a quick or easy victory over communism in the impoverished agrarian world.

2

There are cultural, as well as socio-economic, causes for the remarkable appeal of communism to the agrarian world. The ancient cultures of Asia, whether humanistic, as the Confucianism of China, or mystic as the religions of India, have one common characteristic. They lack historical dynamism. It would be impossible in brief terms to do justice to the various roots of the western historical dynamism as found in the Hebraic faith, in Greek humanism and in the Christian religion. This historical dynamism is partly an attitude toward the whole drama of history, involving a sense of expectancy that something significantly new and meaningful will occur in the future. It is partly derived from an attitude toward nature. This involves a belief that man is to have dominion over nature, which is assumed in Biblical faith and which stands in contrast to a pious awe before nature in Oriental pantheism. It also implies both the idea of the rationality of nature, which the western tradition draws from Greek thought, and the equally necessary idea of contingency in nature, which is drawn from the Christian idea of Creation. These two ideas together furnish the basis for modern science and the scientific "exploitation" of nature. "The method of Galilean science," declares Mr. Michael Foster, ". . . presupposes (a) that it is impossible that nature should not embody a mathematically intelligible scheme and exhibit laws mathematically definable; but (b) that which of the possible alternative schemes it embodies and which of the several laws equally definable it exhibits can be decided only by observation and experiment."[*]

The one idea lays the foundation for the deductive, and the other for the inductive, methods of science. These two together account for the remarkable achievements of western science. They are distinguished from the indifference toward problems of nature in Confucian human-

[*]Michael Foster in *Mind*, Vol. xlv, p. 24 (1936). See also John Baillie, *Natural Science and the Spiritual Life.*

ism and the mystic reverence of nature in Hindu pantheism in which reverence both the rationality and the contingency of natural events are obscured.

In any event the cultures of the Orient are sleeping-waking cultures in which the drama of human history is not taken seriously and in which nature is either deified or reduced to a realm of illusion. Communism is a historically dynamic religion which comes to the hopeless people of the Orient as the harbinger of a great hope. They have been exposed to the culture of the West; but have found the various western cultural and religious exports contradictory. There seemed to be a clear contradiction between the Christian faith, as expounded by the Christian missionary enterprise, and the cult of science as acquired by Oriental students in the academic centers of the West. There seemed also to be a contradiction between the imperial impulses exhibited by western power and the idealism propounded by western religion. There was furthermore no clear political program in western cultural exports. Christianity is reluctant to identify its piety with any particular political program for the very reasons which make such an identification so dangerous in communism. As politics deals with the proximate ends of life, and religion with ultimate ones, it is always a source of illusion if the one is simply invested with the sanctity of the other.

Communism has a tremendous original advantage as a destructive force in the dying sleeping cultures of the Orient because it is not only historically dynamic but it also seems to combine all the impulses of historical dynamism, which so frequently stand in contradiction, into one single unified impulse. This unification is spurious and dangerous; but this fact adds to, rather than detracts from, its striking power. Religion and science are combined in such a way that the modern cult of science is brought completely into the service of an existential faith. "Marxist-Leninist" science has proved to have a great attractive power in the universities of China. And even in India the intellectuals, without political pressure upon them, take its pretensions seriously.

The Marxist "science" does have one advantage over bourgeois social science. The latter usually gives itself to the illusion that reasoning about historical events can be presuppositionless and can achieve the disinterested character of the natural sciences. Yet all thought about human life and destiny and about the problems of man's common existence are "existential" in the sense that they begin and end with presuppositions of faith which are not determined by scientific inquiry. They begin with the interests of the self and they end with some concept of ultimate meaning, some hope or faith in what life is or should be. The communist faith is not only explicitly "existential" as bourgeois science is not. It also provides for an identification of the beginning and the end of the reasoning process which is particularly dear to the human heart. It seeks to prove that the interests of a particular historical force (in this case of the proletariat) are the unqualified instruments of the ultimate. The poor, in communist apocalypse, cannot emancipate themselves from the injustices from which they suffer without emancipating the whole of mankind from all evil. This formulation has proved tremendously attractive to both intellectuals and to industrial workers in some portions of the western world; and it is bound to have an even greater persuasive power in the non-technical societies. To assign a Messianic function in history to the poor not only seems to transmute their resentments into vehicles of the ultimate good; but it also eases the uneasy conscience of those who are affronted by social injustice. As a religion this faith generates what in Christian terms is regarded as the very essence of sin. It identifies the interests of a particular self or of a particular force in history with the final purposes of the God of history. God, in this case, is of course the dialectic which gives meaning to the whole. Such a faith also has an advantage over a cynical creed, such as Nazism. It does not demand that a particular force or interest in history defy every common standard of justice and right in the name of its own ambitions. In theory it defies these standards only provisionally. Ultimately, according to this creed, the ruthless battle of the proletariat against all other forces in history allegedly leads to the triumph of universal justice.

For good measure communism couches this religion in the language of "science" and thus comes to a world, tired of defeatist religions, as an emancipating force. Moreover, this science also promises the technical conquest of nature. This final pretension has no force in the western world since technical achievements are obviously prior to the proclamation of the communist apocalypse. Russian propagandists do indeed seek to prove that their technical inventions have in most cases anticipated ours. But outside of Russia the facts are too obvious to give these pretensions any force, even among prospective devotees.

Thus, every aspect of the cultural crisis in the sleeping cultures of the Orient combines with the socio-historic tension between poor and rich nations to give this spurious religion a tremendous plausibility and attractive power. This ironic situation is heightened by the fact that the ethos in our technical and democratic world, more particularly in the highly favored American nation, is so different from that of the world in which these illusions arise that it is difficult for us to appreciate their force in the impoverished world. Our difficulties are heightened by a widespread tendency in western social science to seek the comprehension of the social and political phenomena of our era in dimensions bordering upon the purely biological. We confront manias and confusions in the world, at enmity with us, which certainly lead to very stubborn forms of "aggressiveness." But this aggressiveness is compounded of spiritual, historical, social and cultural forces which cannot be measured by our computations taken from biology. We are in danger, therefore, of facing the international "class struggle" with an uncomprehending fury or complete dismay.

3

The attractive power of communism in the impoverished world is heightened by the lack of receptivity in this world for almost every facet of what we know as democracy. Democracy in the West is both a political system and a way of life. It requires a high degree of literacy among its citizens, a sense of the dignity of the individual but also a sense of his responsibility to a wider community than his family. The bourgeois versions of the concept of the dignity of the individual are frequently defective. Sometimes they unduly subordinate the sense of community to the idea of the worth of the individual; sometimes they illicitly identify the dignity with the virtue of the individual. Therefore our preaching of democracy frequently seems highly irrelevant to broken or partially reconstructed communities who are desperately seeking for a viable structure for their common life.

But even without these particular defects, democracy in its most ideal formulation is not as immediately relevant to the ancient cultures of the East or to the primitive cultures of Africa as is generally supposed. Some of both the spiritual and the socio-economic presuppositions for it are lacking. Spiritually the Orient is informed by religions which are either mystic and pantheistic such as Buddhism and Hinduism; or humanistic and collectivist such as the Confucianism of China or the Shintoism of Japan. Pantheistic religions can find no significance for the individual in the integral unity of his spiritual and physical life. The purpose of religious redemption is the annulment of individual existence and its incorporation into a divine unity. It is a far cry from this kind of mysticism to the sober, earthbound humanism of Confucianism. There are no greater differences between East and West than between the humanism of China and the mysticism of India. But Chinese humanism does not, for this reason, offer the individual a more significant place in the scheme of things. His life is oriented to the family.

All social relations and moral ideals (Confucius' "Five Relations") are derived from the family. Japan was able to achieve a more solid national cohesion because Shintoism establishes the whole nation as a kind of large family, related to a divine ancestor. But in either case the individual does not arrive at a position of independence from the group. In Confucianism the group to which the life of the individual is oriented remains the family, through all the vicissitudes of a rich cultural history. Therefore the national cohesion always remained precarious and unstable.

There is thus no spiritual basis in the Orient for what we know as the "dignity of the individual." This is one reason why there is little prospect in China for heroic resistance to totalitarianism, when once established. Much was made, before communism triumphed in China, of the alleged power of Confucianism to absorb every cultural force which may gain a provisional triumph over it. But since communism has triumphed in China we hear less of this alleged stubborn vitality of Confucianism. Its lack of historical dynamism makes it an easy prey to communism, particularly among the youth; and the lack of individual independence and the strong emphasis upon prudential rather than heroic virtue, predisposes even opponents of communism to bow to its power. The mystic religions of the Orient will hardly prove more capable of offering spiritual resistance to the demonic dynamism of the communist movement.

A democratic society requires some capacity of the individual both to defy social authority on occasion when its standards violate his conscience and to relate himself to larger and larger communities than the primary family group. The highly developed individual self-consciousness in the western Christian tradition is supported by a long spiritual history. Yet, even in the West, it did not come to full flower until the developments of a commercial and industrial civilization broke the organic forms of western feudalism. The complex and multiple communities of modern society involved the individual in both complementary and contradictory loyalties and thus created a new degree of individual independence. At the same time technical developments increased the possibility of communications so that the broader community would be held together not merely by political authority but by spiritual and cultural cohesions. The varied skills of technical society and its more mobile and flexible forms of property also emancipated the individual from the restraints of hereditary property and vocation.

A democratic society, in short, requires not only a spiritual and cultural basis which is lacking in the Orient but a socio-economic foundation which primitive and traditional civilizations cannot quickly acquire. Many of the values of democratic society which are most highly prized in the West are, therefore, neither understood nor desired outside of the orbit of western society. Resentment against feudal injustice easily prompts the youth of decaying feudal societies to espouse the cause of a new collectivist culture, which promises justice. They do not understand the tyrannical consequences of this new form of totalitarianism. But even if they did understand, they cannot be expected to feel the loss of liberty with the same sense of grievous deprivation as in the West.

126

4

If we consider both the cultural and the socio-economic hazards to any immediate success of democracy in the non-technical world and rightly gauge the causes for the attractive power of communism in this world, we are driven to the conclusion that we must face the menace of the spread of tyranny in the non-industrial world for many decades to come. We will not, of course, fail to take the strategic and military measures which are possible and necessary to arrest its growth. But we will avoid the hysteria which arises from the mistaken belief that this growth is due merely to some political or strategic miscalculation by this or that government agency or administration. Fortunately the non-industrial world lacks the technical resources to offer a mortal challenge to our security. Fortunately, also, there are genuine spiritual and moral affinities between ourselves and Japan and the Philippines, which will make it possible to hold the "island littoral" in the Pacific, though the danger of communist infiltration into even these Asian cultures must not be obscured.

But these tactical and strategic measures and possibilities must not make us oblivious to the larger pattern of history. In that larger pattern we face a revolt of impoverished peoples of the world against the centers of technical power in which justified and unjustified resentments are so curiously mingled, and legitimate desires for greater well-being are so inextricably intertwined with illusory hopes that decades upon decades will be required to bring order out of this chaos. There is no wisdom in the constant iterations of slogans in which liberty is contrasted with tyranny; and in which this tyranny is so defined that the utopian illusions, which nourish it, are obscured. Communism is not merely another version of Nazism. Nazism was a morally cynical creed which defied every norm of justice. It represented a moral nihilism which could have developed only in the decay of a highly developed and sophisticated civilization. Communism is a morally utopian creed which has a much wider appeal than Nazism because it speaks in the name of justice rather than in defiance of justice; and it is ostensibly devoted to the establishment of a universal society, rather than to the supremacy of a race or nation. The fact that its illusory hopes are capable of generating cruelties and tyrannies, exceeding even those of a cynical creed, can be understood only if it is realized how much more plausible and dangerous the corruption of the good can be in human history than explicit evil.

The rise of communism in our world is comparable to the rise of Islam and its challenge of Christian civilization in the high Middle Ages. Some of the measures we take against it are informed by the same lack of realism which characterized the Crusades. The Islamic power finally waned. It was destroyed not so much by its foes as by its own inner corruptions. The Sultan of Turkey found it ultimately impossible to support the double role of political head of a nation and the spiritual head of the Islamic world. Stalin has this same double role in the world of communist religion. He or his successors will finally be convicted of insinuating the power impulses of a Russian state into the Messianic illusions of an osten--

sibly world-wide political religion. If we fully understand the deep springs which feed the illusions of this religion, the nature of the social resentments which nourish them and the realities of life which must ultimately refute them, we might acquire the necessary patience to wait out the long run of history while we take such measures as are necessary to combat the more immediate perils.

CHAPTER VII

The American Future

1

NATIONS, as individuals, may be assailed by contradictory temptations. They may be tempted to flee the responsibilities of their power or refuse to develop their potentialities. But they may also refuse to recognize the limits of their possibilities and seek greater power than is given to mortals. Naturally there are no fixed limits for the potentialities of men or nations. There is therefore no nice line to be drawn between a normal expression of human creativity and either the sloth which refuses to assume the responsibilities of human freedom or the pride which overestimates man's individual or collective power. But it is possible to discern extreme forms of each evil very clearly; and also to recognize various shades of evil between the extremes and the norm.

The temptation to disavow the responsibilities of human freedom or to leave human potentialities undeveloped usually assails the weak, rather than the strong. In the Biblical parable it was the "one talent" man who "hid his treasure in the ground." Our nation ought, therefore, not to take too much credit for having mastered a temptation which assailed us for several decades. It was a rather unique historical phenomenon that a nation with our potentialities should have been tempted to isolationism and withdrawal from world responsibilities. Various factors contributed to the persuasiveness of the temptation. We were so strong and our continental security seemed so impregnable (on cursory glance at least) that we were encouraged in the illusion that we could live our own life without too much regard for a harassed world. Our sense of superior virtue over the alleged evils of European civilization and our fear of losing our innocency if we braved the tumults of world politics, added spiritual vanity to ignoble prudence as the second cause of our irresponsibility. We thought we might keep ourselves free of the evils of a warring world and thus preserve a healthy civilization, amidst the expected doom of a decrepit one. This hope of furnishing the seed-corn for a new beginning persuaded moral idealists to combine with cynical realists in propounding the policy of power without responsibility.

However, human life is healthy only in relationship; and modern technical achievements have accentuated the interdependence of men and of nations. It therefore became apparent, that we could neither be really secure in an insecure world nor find life worth living if we bought our security at the price of civilization's doom. This knowledge came to us during and after the Second World War and marked a fateful turning point in our national life. Some of our friends and allies still profess uncertainty

131

about the reality of our conversion from an irresponsible to a responsible relation to the community of nations. But, whatever may be our future errors, it is fairly safe to predict that we have finally triumphed over the temptation to "hide our talent in the ground."

We will not, however, take too much credit for this achievement if we remember that the temptation, over which we triumphed, is one which assails the weak rather than the strong. Indeed, a part of the resource for our triumph was our gradual realization that we were not weak, but strong; that we had in fact become very strong.

Significantly the same world which only yesterday feared our possible return to adolescent irresponsibility is now exercised about the possibilities of the misuse of our power. We would do well to understand the legitimacy of such fears rather than resent their seeming injustice. It is characteristic of human nature, whether in its individual or collective expression, that it has no possibility of exercising power, without running the danger of overestimating the purity of the wisdom which directs it. The apprehensions of allies and friends is, therefore, but a natural human reaction to what men intuitively know to be the temptations of power. A European statesman stated the issue very well recently in the words: "We are grateful to America for saving us from communism. But our gratitude does not prevent us from fearing that we might become an American colony. That danger lies in the situation of America's power and Europe's weakness." The statesman, when reminded of the strain of genuine idealism in American life, replied: "The idealism does indeed prevent America from a gross abuse of its power.

132

But it might well accentuate the danger Europeans confront. For American power in the service of American idealism could create a situation in which we would be too impotent to correct you when you are wrong and you would be too idealistic to correct yourself."

Such a measured judgment upon the virtues and perils of America's position in the world community accurately describes the hazards of our position in the world. Our moral perils are not those of conscious malice or the explicit lust for power. They are the perils which can be understood only if we realize the ironic tendency of virtues to turn into vices when too complacently relied upon; and of power to become vexatious if the wisdom which directs it is trusted too confidently. The ironic elements in American history can be overcome, in short, only if American idealism comes to terms with the limits of all human striving, the fragmentariness of all human wisdom, the precariousness of all historic configurations of power, and the mixture of good and evil in all human virtue. America's moral and spiritual success in relating itself creatively to a world community requires, not so much a guard against the gross vices, about which the idealists warn us, as a reorientation of the whole structure of our idealism. That idealism is too oblivious of the ironic perils to which human virtue, wisdom and power are subject. It is too certain that there is a straight path toward the goal of human happiness; too confident of the wisdom and idealism which prompt men and nations toward that goal; and too blind to the curious compounds of good and evil in which the actions of the best men and nations abound.

2

The two aspects of our historic situation which tend particularly to aggravate the problems of American idealism are: (a) That American power in the present world situation is inordinately great; (b) that the contemporary international situation offers no clear road to the achievement of either peace or victory over tyranny. The first aspect embodies perils to genuine community between ourselves and our allies; for power generates both justified and unjustified fears and resentments among the relatively powerless. The second aspect embodies the temptation to become impatient and defiant of the slow and sometimes contradictory processes of history. We may be too secure in both our sense of power and our sense of virtue to be ready to engage in a patient chess game with the recalcitrant forces of historic destiny. We could bring calamity upon ourselves and the world by forgetting that even the most powerful nations and even the wisest planners of the future remain themselves creatures as well as creators of the historical process. Man cannot rise to a simple triumph over historical fate.

In considering the perils of our inordinate power it would be well to concede that it embodies some real advantages for the world community. It is quite possible that if power had been more evenly distributed in the non-communist world the degree of cohesion actually attained would have been difficult. Many national communities gained their first triumph over chaos by the organizing energy of one particular power, sufficiently dominant to suppress the confusion of competing forces.

Thus, dominant city-states in Egypt and in Mesopotamia were responsible for the order and cohesion of these first great empires of human history. The preponderant power of America may have a similar role to play in the present international scene. There is, furthermore, a youthful belief in historic possibilities in our American culture, a confidence that problems can be solved, which frequently stands in creative contrast with the spiritual tiredness of many European nations as also with the defeatism of Oriental cultures. Our hegemonic position in the world community rests upon a buoyant vigor as well as upon our preponderant economic power.

Nevertheless, great disproportions of power are as certainly moral hazards to justice and community as they are foundations of minimal order. They are hazards to community both because they arouse resentments and fears among those who have less power; and because they tempt the strong to wield their power without too much consideration of the interests and views of those upon whom it impinges. Modern democratic nations have sought to bring power into the service of justice in three ways. (a) They have tried to distribute economic and political power and prevent its undue concentration. (b) They have tried to bring it under social and moral review. (c) They have sought to establish inner religious and moral checks upon it.

Of these three methods the first is not relevant to the international community, as at present inchoately organized. The relative power of particular nations must be accepted as fateful historic facts about which little can be done. The idealists who imagine that these dis-

135

proportions of power would be dissolved in a global constitutional system do not understand the realities of the political order. No world government could possibly possess, for generations to come, the moral and political authority to redistribute power between the nations in the degree in which highly cohesive national communities have accomplished this end in recent centuries. Furthermore, even the most healthy modern nations must be content with only approximate equilibria of power lest they destroy the vitalities of various social forces by a too rigorous effort to bring the whole communal life under an equalitarian discipline. The preponderance of American power is thus an inexorable fact for decades to come, whether within or without a fuller world constitution than now prevails. If it does disappear it will be eliminated by the emergence of new forces or the new coalition of older forces, rather than by constitutional contrivance.

The strategy of bringing power under social and political review is a possibility for the international community, even in its present nascent form. It is a wholesome development for America and the world that the United Nations is becoming firmly established, not so much as an institution, capable of bridging the chasm between the communist and the non-communist world (in which task it can have only minimal success), but as an organ in which even the most powerful of the democratic nations must bring their policies under the scrutiny of world public opinion. Thus inevitable aberrations, arising from the pride of power, are corrected. It will be even more hopeful for the peace and justice of the world community, if a fragmented Europe should gain the unity to speak with more unanimity in the councils of the nations than is now possible. It is impossible for any nation or individual fully to understand the peculiar circumstances and the unique history of any other nation or individual, which create their special view of reality. It is important, therefore, that the fragmentary wisdom of any nation should be prevented from achieving the bogus omniscience, which occurs when the weak are too weak to dare challenge the opinion of the powerful. Such a tyrannical situation not only within, but between, the communist nations must finally destroy the community of that world.

It is also to be hoped that the Asian world will gain sufficient voice in the councils of the free nations to correct the inevitable bias of western nations in the same manner.

It is now generally acknowledged (to give an example of the salutary character of such discipline) that American policy in regard to the rearmament of Germany was too precipitate and too indifferent toward certain moral and political hazards of which Europe was conscious in that undertaking. There were, on the other hand, fears in Europe which might have prevented the inclusion of Western Germany in the full community of the noncommunist world and the concomitant grant of the right, and acknowledgment of the responsibility, of common defense of that community. The tolerable solution of this problem was achieved by compromises between the American and the European position. Thus a creative synthesis was achieved despite the hazards of disproportionate power.

If there should be, as many Europeans believe, too great a preoccupation in America with the task of winning a war which Europe wants to avoid; and if there should be in Europe, as some Americans believe, so desperate a desire to avoid war that the danger is run of bringing on the conflict by lack of resolution, it is to be hoped that a similar creative synthesis of complementary viewpoints will take place. The real test of such a synthesis will occur at the point in time when American preparedness has reached its highest possibility and the fear of the rapid outmoding of modern weapons and the consequent economic burden of ever-new preparedness efforts might tempt American strategists to welcome a final joining of the issue. In that situation many Americans would, of course, strongly resist the temptation to embark upon a preventive war. But their resolution will be strengthened and their cause have a better prospect of success if the decision lies not with one powerful nation but with a real community of nations.

The third strategy of disciplining the exercise of power, that of an inner religious and moral check, is usually interpreted to mean the cultivation of a sense of justice. The inclination "to give each man his due" is indeed one of the ends of such a discipline. But a sense of humility which recognizes that nations are even more incapable than individuals of fully understanding the rights and claims of others may be an even more important element in such a discipline. A too confident sense of justice always leads to injustice. In so far as men and nations are "judges in their own case" they are bound to betray the human weakness of having a livelier sense of their own

138

interest than of the competing interest. That is why "just" men and nations may easily become involved in ironic refutations of their moral pretensions.

Genuine community, whether between men or nations, is not established merely through the realization that we need one another, though indeed we do. That realization alone may still allow the strong to use the lives of the weaker as instruments of their own self-realization. Genuine community is established only when the knowledge that we need one another is supplemented by the recognition that "the other," that other form of life, or that other unique community is the limit beyond which our ambitions must not run and the boundary beyond which our life must not expand.

It is significant that most genuine community is established below and above the level of conscious moral idealism. Below that level we find the strong forces of nature and nature-history, sex and kinship, common language and geographically determined togetherness, operative. Above the level of idealism the most effective force of community is religious humility. This includes the charitable realization that the vanities of the other group or person, from which we suffer, is not different in kind, though possibly in degree, from similar vanities in our own life. It also includes a religious sense of the mystery and greatness of the other life, which we violate if we seek to comprehend it too simply from our standpoint.

Such resources of community are of greater importance in our nation today than abstract constitutional schemes, of which our idealists are so fond. Most of these schemes will be proved, upon close examination, to be indifferent

139

toward the urgencies and anxieties which nations, less favored than we, experience; and to betray sentimentalities about the perplexing problems of human togetherness in which only the powerful and the secure can indulge.

3

The second characteristic of the contemporary situation, which challenges American idealism, is that there are no guarantees either for the victory of democracy over tyranny or for a peaceful solution of the fateful conflict between two great centers of power. We have previously noted how the tragic dilemmas and the pathetic uncertainties and frustrations of contemporary history offer ironic refutation of the dreams of happiness and virtue of a liberal age and, especially, of the American hopes. Escape from our ironic situation obviously demands that we moderate our conceptions of the ability of men and of nations to discern the future; and of the power of even great nations to bring a tortuous historical process to, what seems to them, a logical and proper conclusion.

The difficulty of our own powerful nation in coming to terms with the frustrations of history, and our impatience with a situation which requires great exertions without the promise of certain success, is quite obviously symbolic of the whole perplexity of modern culture. The perplexity arises from the fact that men have been preoccupied with man's capacity to master historical forces and have forgotten that the same man, including the collective man embodied in powerful nations, is also a creature of these historical forces. Since man is a creator, endowed with a unique freedom, he "looks before and after and pines for what is not." He envisages goals and ends of life which are not dictated by the immediate necessities of life. He builds and surveys the great cultural and social structures of his day, recognizes the plight in which they become involved and devises various means and ends to extricate his generation from such a plight. He would not be fully human if he did not lift himself above his immediate hour, if he felt neither responsibility for the future weal of his civilization, nor gratitude for the whole glorious and tragic drama of human history, culminating in the present moment.

But it is easy to forget that even the most powerful nation or alliance of nations is merely one of many forces in the historical drama; and that the conflict of many wills and purposes, which constitute that drama, give it a bizarre pattern in which it is difficult to discern a real meaning. It is even more difficult to subject it to a preconceived order. We have previously considered the ironic nature of the fact that the chief force of recalcitrance against the hopes of a democratic world should be furnished by a political religion, the animus of whose recalcitrance should be derived from its fanatic belief that it can reduce all historical forces to its conception of a rational order. The fact that this religion should have a special appeal to decaying feudal societies, which have been left behind in the march of technical progress of the western world is one of those imponderable factors in history, which no one could have foreseen but which can be countered only if we do not try too simply to overcome the ambivalence and hesitancies of the non-technical world by the display of our power, or the claim of superiority for our "way of life."

We have enough discernment as creators of history to know that there is a certain "logic" in its course. We know that recently the development of an inchoate world community requires that it acquire global political organs for the better integration of its life. But if we imagine that we can easily transmute this logic into historical reality we will prove ourselves blind to the limitations of man as creature of history. For the achievement of a constitutional world order is frustrated not merely by the opposition of a resolute foe who has his own conception of such an order. It is impeded also by the general limitations of man as creature. The most important of these is the fact that human communities are never purely artifacts of the human mind and will. Human communities are subject to "organic" growth. This means that they cannot deny their relation to "nature"; for the force of their cohesion is partly drawn from the necessities of nature (kinship, geography, etc.) rather than from the realm of freedom. Even when it is not pure nature but historic tradition and common experience which provides the cement of cohesion, the integrating force is still not in the realm of pure freedom or the fruit of pure volition. Thus, the "Atlantic community" is becoming a reality partly because it does have common cultural inheritances and partly because the exigencies of history are forcing mutual tasks upon it. The assumption of these mutual responsibilities requires a whole series of clear decisions. Yet it is not possible even for such a limited international community to be constituted into an integral community by one clear act of political will. Naturally a more unlimited or global community, with fewer common cultural traditions to bind it and less immediate urgencies to force difficult decisions upon a reluctant human will, will have even greater difficulty in achieving stable political cohesion.

All these matters are understood intuitively by practical statesmen who know from experience that the mastery of historical destiny is a tortuous process in which powerful forces may be beguiled, deflected, and transmuted but never simply annulled or defied. The difficulty, particularly in America, is that the wisdom of this practical statesmanship is so frequently despised as foolishness by the supposedly more "idealistic" science of our age. Thus the conscience of our nation is confused to the point of schizophrenia; and the inevitable disappointments, frustrations and illogicalities of world politics are wrongly interpreted as nothing but the fruit of "unscientific" blundering. A nation with an inordinate degree of political power is doubly tempted to exceed the bounds of historical possibilities, if it is informed by an idealism which does not understand the limits of man's wisdom and volition in history.

4

The recognition of historical limits must not, however, lead to a betrayal of cherished values and historical attainments. Historical pragmatism exists on the edge of opportunism, but cannot afford to fall into the abyss. The difficulty of sustaining the values of a free world must not prompt us, for instance, to come to terms with tyranny. Nor must the perplexities confronting the task of achieving global community betray us into a complacent acceptance of national loyalty as the final moral possibility of history. It is even more grievously wrong either to bow to "waves of the future" or to yield to inertias of the past than to seek illusory escape from historical difficulties by utopian dreams.

Through the whole course of history mankind has, by a true spiritual instinct, reserved its highest admiration for those heroes who resisted evil at the risk or price of fortune and life without too much hope of success. Sometimes their very indifference to the issue of success or failure provided the stamina which made success possible. Sometimes the heroes of faith perished outside the promised land. This paradoxical relation between the possible and the impossible in history proves that the frame of history is wider than the nature-time in which it is grounded. The injunction of Christ: "Fear not them which kill the body, but are not able to kill the soul" (Matthew 10:28) neatly indicates the dimension of human existence which transcends the basis which human life and history have in nature. Not merely in Christian thought but in the noblest paganism, it has been understood that a too desperate desire to preserve life or to gain obvious success must rob life of its meaning. If this be so, there cannot be a simple correlation betwen virtue and happiness, or between immediate and ultimate success.

While collective man lacks the capacity of individual man to sacrifice "the body" (*i.e.* historical security) for an end which may not be historically validated, yet nations have proved capable of great sacrifice in defending their liberties against tyranny, for instance. The tendency of a liberal culture to regard the highest human possibilities as capable of simple historical attainment, and to interpret all tragic and contradictory elements in the pattern of history as merely provisional, has immersed the spirit of our age in a sentimentality which so uncritically identifies idealism with prudence that it can find no place in its scheme of things for heroic action or heroic patience. Yet the only possibility of success for our nation and our culture in achieving the historic goals of peace and justice lies in our capacity to make sacrifices and to sustain endeavors without complete certainty of success.

We could not bear the burdens required to save the world from tyranny if there were no prospects of success. The necessity of this measure of historic hope marks the spiritual stature of collective, as distinguished from individual, man. Even among individuals only few individuals are able to rise to the height of heroic nonchalance about historic possibilities. But while the nation cannot fulfill its mission in a given situation without some prospect of success, it also cannot persist in any great endeavor if it is so preoccupied with immediate historic possibilities that it is constantly subjected to distracting alternations of illusion and disillusion.

The fact that the European nations, more accustomed to the tragic vicissitudes of history, still have a measure of misgiving about our leadership in the world community is due to their fear that our "technocratic" tendency to equate the mastery of nature with the mastery of history could tempt us to lose patience with the tortuous course of history. We might be driven to hysteria by its inevitable frustrations. We might be tempted to bring the whole of modern history to a tragic conclusion by one final and mighty effort to overcome its frustrations. The political term for such an effort is "preventive war." It is not an immediate temptation; but it could become so in the next decade or two.

A democracy can not of course, engage in an explicit preventive war. But military leadership can heighten crises to the point where war becomes unavoidable.

The power of such a temptation to a nation, long accustomed to expanding possibilities and only recently subjected to frustration, is enhanced by the spiritual aberrations which arise in a situation of intense enmity. The certainty of the foe's continued intransigence seems to be the only fixed fact in an uncertain future. Nations find it even more difficult than individuals to preserve sanity when confronted with a resolute and unscrupulous foe. Hatred disturbs all residual serenity of spirit and vindictiveness muddies every pool of sanity. In the present situation even the sanest of our statesmen have found it convenient to conform their policies to the public temper of fear and hatred which the most vulgar of our politicians have generated or exploited. Our foreign policy is thus threatened with a kind of apoplectic rigidity and inflexibility. Constant proof is required that the foe is hated with sufficient vigor. Unfortunately the only persuasive proof seems to be the disavowal of precisely those discriminate judgments which are so necessary for an effective conflict with the evil, which we are supposed to abhor. There is no simple triumph over this spirit of fear and hatred. It is certainly an achievement beyond the resources of a simple idealism. For naïve idealists are always so preoccupied with their own virtues that they have no residual awareness of the common characteristics in all human foibles and frailties and could not bear to be reminded that there is a hidden kinship between the vices of even the most vicious and the virtues of even the most upright.

5

The American situation is such a vivid symbol of the spiritual perplexities of modern man, because the degree of American power tends to generate illusions to which a technocratic culture is already too prone. This technocratic approach to problems of history, which erroneously equates the mastery of nature with the mastery of historical destiny, in turn accentuates a very old failing in human nature: the inclination of the wise, or the powerful, or the virtuous, to obscure and deny the human limitations in all human achievements and pretensions.

The most rigorous and searching criticism of the weaknesses in our foreign policy, which may be ascribed to the special character of our American idealism, has recently been made by one of our most eminent specialists in foreign policy, Mr. George Kennan.*

He ascribes the weaknesses of our policy to a too simple "legalistic-moralistic" approach and defines this approach as informed by an uncritical reliance upon moral and constitutional schemes, and by too little concern for

*George F. Kennan, *American Diplomacy*, 1900–1950.

the effect of our policy upon other nations, and too little anticipation of the possible disruption of policies by incalculable future occurrences. In short, he accuses the nation of pretending too much prescience of an unknown future and of an inclination to regard other peoples "in our own image." These are, of course, precisely the perils to which all human idealism is subject and which our great power and our technocratic culture have aggravated.

Mr. Kennan's solution for our problem is to return to the policy of making the "national interest" the touchstone of our diplomacy. He does not intend to be morally cynical in the advocacy of this course. He believes that a modest awareness that our own interests represent the limit of our competence should prompt such a policy. His theory is that we may know what is good for us but should be less certain that we know what is good for others. This admonition to modesty is valid as far as it goes. Yet his solution is wrong. For egotism is not the proper cure for an abstract and pretentious idealism.

Since the lives and interests of other men and communities always impinge upon our own, a preoccupation with our own interests must lead to an illegitimate indifference toward the interests of others, even when modesty prompts the preoccupation. The cure for a pretentious idealism, which claims to know more about the future and about other men than is given mortal man to know, is not egotism. It is a concern for both the self and the other in which the self, whether individual or collective, preserves a "decent respect for the opinions of mankind," derived from a modest awareness of the limits of its own knowledge and power.

It is not an accident of history that a culture which made so much of humanity and humaneness should have generated such frightful inhumanities; and that these inhumanities are not limited to the explicitly fanatic politico-religious movements. Mr. Kennan rightly points to the evils which arise from the pursuit of unlimited rather than limited ends, even by highly civilized nations in the modern era. The inhumanities of our day, which modern tryannies exhibit in the nth degree, are due to an idealism in which reason is turned into unreason because it is not conscious of the contingent character of the presuppositions with which the reasoning process begins, and in which idealism is transmuted into inhumanity because the idealist seeks to comprehend the whole realm of ends from his standpoint.

A nice symbol of this difficulty in the policy of even "just" nations is the ironic embarrassment in which the victorious democracies became involved in their program of "demilitarizing" the vanquished "militaristic" nations. In Japan they encouraged a ridiculous article in the new constitution which committed the nation to a perpetual pacifist defenselessness. In less than half a decade they were forced to ask their "demilitarized" former foes to rearm, and become allies in a common defense against a new foe, who had recently been their victorious ally.

We cannot expect even the wisest of nations to escape every peril of moral and spiritual complacency; for nations have always been constitutionally self-righteous. But it will make a difference whether the culture in which the policies of nations are formed is only as deep and as high as the nation's highest ideals; or whether there is a dimension in the culture from the standpoint of which the element of vanity in all human ambitions and achievements is discerned. But this is a height which can be grasped only by faith; for everything that is related in terms of simple rational coherence with the ideals of a culture or a nation will prove in the end to be a simple justification of its most cherished values. The God before whom "the nations are as a drop in the bucket and are counted as small dust in the balances" is known by faith and not by reason. The realm of mystery and meaning which encloses and finally makes sense out of the baffling configurations of history is not identical with any scheme of rational intelligibility. The faith which appropriates the meaning in the mystery inevitably involves an experience of repentance for the false meanings which the pride of nations and cultures introduces into the pattern. Such repentance is the true source of charity; and we are more desperately in need of genuine charity than of more technocratic skills.

CHAPTER VIII

The Significance of Irony

1

ANY interpretation of historical patterns and configurations raises the question whether the patterns, which the observer discerns, are "objectively" true or are imposed upon the vast stuff of history by his imagination. History might be likened to the confusion of spots on the cards used by psychiatrists in a Rorschach test. The patient is asked to report what he sees in these spots; and he may claim to find the outlines of an elephant, butterfly or frog. The psychiatrist draws conclusions from these judgments about the state of the patient's imagination rather than about the actual configuration of spots on the card. Are historical patterns equally subjective?

Is the discernment of an ironic element in the history of the American nation or of modern culture merely the fruit of a capricious imagination? Is the pattern of irony superimposed upon the historical data which are so various that they would be tolerant of almost any pattern, which the observer might care to impose? In answering such questions one must admit the subjective element in historical judgments, but also insist upon the distinction between

151

purely arbitrary judgments and those which throw real light upon the variegated events of history. Patterns of meaning are arbitrary if they do violence to the facts, or single out correlations or sequences of events, which are so fortuitous that only some special interest or passion could persuade the observer of the significance of the correlation. An example of such caprice was recently given by a politician who compared the number of people under communist rule in 1932 with the number in 1950. He drew the conclusion that the vast increase in the number of communist-dominated peoples (an increase which was made particularly impressive by the addition of millions of Chinese to the total) was evidence of the complicity of the "New Deal" in the spread of communism. Such conclusions can be advanced only from the standpoint of an obvious bias, and are credible only to an equally biased mind.

It is possible, however, to interpret the endless and variegated events and sequences of history from many legitimate standpoints which are not corrupted by special interest. But the question is whether the interpretations have any legitimacy or credibility to the observer apart from his acceptance of the governing principle of interpretation which prompted the generalizations. To be specific, is an ironic interpretation of current history generally plausible; or does its credibility depend upon a Christian view of history in which the ironic view seems to be particularly grounded?

One must answer that question by insisting that there are elements in current history so obviously ironic that they must be patent to any observer who fulfills the conditions required for the detection of irony. Nevertheless, the consistency with which the category of the ironic is applied to historical events does finally depend upon a governing faith or world view.

There are so many obviously ironic elements in current history, particularly in our own national history, because a nation which has risen so quickly from weakness to power and from innocency to responsibility and which meets a foe who has transmuted our harmless illusions into noxious ones is bound to be involved in rather ironic incongruities.

These ironic contrasts and incongruities, though obvious, are not always observed because irony cannot be directly experienced. The knowledge of it depends upon an observer who is not so hostile to the victim of irony as to deny the element of virtue which must constitute a part of the ironic situation; nor yet so sympathetic as to discount the weakness, the vanity and pretension which constitute another element. Since the participant in an ironic situation cannot, unless he be very self-critical, fulfill this latter condition, the knowledge of irony is usually reserved for observers rather than participants. If participants in an ironic situation become conscious of the vanities and illusions which make an ironic situation more than merely comic, they would tend to abate the pretensions and dissolve the irony. Purely hostile observers, on the other hand, may laugh bitterly at the comedy in an ironic situation, but they could not admit the virtue in the intentions which miscarry so comically.

Individuals do, of course, have a degree of transcendence over the vicissitudes of their nations and communities, no matter how intimately they are involved in them. They may, therefore, be individual observers of an ironic situation in which they are collectively involved.

Ironic contrasts and incongruities have an element of the comic in them in so far as they exhibit absurd juxtapositions of strength and weakness; of wisdom through foolishness; or foolishness as the fruit of wisdom; of guilt arising from the pretensions of innocency; or innocency hiding behind ostensible guilt. Yet contrasts are ironic only if they are not merely absurd, but have a hidden meaning. They must elicit not merely laughter but a knowing smile. The hidden meaning is supplied by the fact that the juxtapositions and contrasts are not merely fortuitous. They are related to each other by some foible of the person who is involved in both. The powerful person who is proved to be really weak is involved in an ironic contrast only if his weakness is due to some pretension of strength. If "pride cometh before the fall," the fall is ironic only if pride contributed to it. A wise person may be ignorant in some areas of life, without his ignorance being ironic. It is so only if the ignorance is derived from the pretension of wisdom.

Ironic transfigurations of weakness, foolishness and sin have the same logic as ironic refutations of power, wisdom and virtue. There is no irony in a purely fortuitous escape of a guilty man from punishment. But it is ironic if those who are despised by their fellowmen achieve recognition and justification in some higher court through the very qualities which brought about their original condemnation; or when the naïveté of babes or simpletons becomes the source of wisdom withheld from the wise.

Comic incongruity is transmuted into irony, when one element in the contrast is found to be the source of the other.

Since ironic interpretations are difficult for reasons already mentioned they are naturally rare in history. The combination of critical, but not hostile, detachment, which is required for their detection, is only infrequently attained.

Yet the Christian faith tends to make the ironic view of human evil in history the normative one. Its conception of redemption from evil carries it beyond the limits of irony, but its interpretation of the nature of evil in human history is consistently ironic. This consistency is achieved on the basis of the belief that the whole drama of human history is under the scrutiny of a divine judge who laughs at human pretensions without being hostile to human aspirations. The laughter at the pretensions is the divine judgment. The judgment is transmuted into mercy if it results in abating the pretensions and in prompting men to a contrite recognition of the vanity of their imagination.

The Biblical interpretation of the human situation is ironic, rather than tragic or pathetic, because of its unique formulation of the problem of human freedom. According to this faith man's freedom does not require his heroic and tragic defiance of the forces of nature. He is not necessarily involved in tragedy in his effort to be truly human. But neither is he necessarily involved in evil because of his relation to the necessities and contingencies of the world of nature. His situation is, therefore, not comprehended as a pathetic imprisonment in the confusion of nature. The evil in human history is regarded as the consequence of man's wrong use of his unique capacities. The wrong use is always due to some failure to recognize the limits of his capacities of power, wisdom and virtue. Man is an ironic creature because he forgets that he is not simply a creator but also a creature.

The Biblical conception of man's unique freedom, which distinguishes him from the other creatures, assumes his right to have dominion over nature and to make natural forces serve human ends. Man is, therefore, not involved in guilt merely by asserting his creative capacities. This emphasis must be distinguished from the motif in the Promethean theme of Greek tragedy. In Æschylus' *Prometheus Bound* Zeus is jealous of Prometheus because the latter seeks to help men to achieve their true humanity by elaborating the arts of civilization. Prometheus declares: "the secret treasure of the earth, all benefits to men, copper, iron, silver, gold . . . who but I could boast of their discovery? No one, I ween, except in idle boasting. Nay, hear the matter in one word: All human arts are from Prometheus."*

According to such a conception every achievement of human culture inevitably implies the HYBRIS which brings the wrath of Zeus upon the human agent. This interpretation makes life fundamentally tragic. The tragic hero elicits the pity and admiration of both Æschylus and the reader because he consciously defies the divine wrath for the sake of achieving a full human creativity. But it is apparent that the power of Zeus is essentially that of the order of nature. Man becomes involved in evil

*Æschylus, *Prometheus Bound*, 490–500.

by breaking the harmonies of nature and exceeding its ends.

Since modern technical achievements include the development of atomic energy and this development has put an almost unmanageable destructiveness into the hands of men, this purely tragic view of human freedom seems to have acquired a new plausibility.

Nevertheless, a purely tragic view of life is not finally viable. It is, at any rate, not the Christian view. According to that view destructiveness is not an inevitable consequence of human creativity. It is not invariably necessary to do evil in order that we may do good. There are, of course, tragic moments and tragic choices in life. There are situations in which a choice must be made between equally valid loyalties and one value must be sacrificed to another. The contest between Antigone and Creon, for instance, was tragic because each from his own perspective, Creon from the standpoint of the state and Antigone from that of the family, was right. All rational resolutions of such tragic dilemmas which pretend that a higher loyalty is necessarily inclusive of a lower one, or that a prudent compromise between competing values can always be found, are false. We have already observed the tragic character of the dilemma which modern democratic nations face, when forced to risk atomic warfare in order to avoid the outbreak of war. The alternatives to this dilemma, proposed by moralists and idealists of various types, will prove upon close scrutiny to involve a dubious sacrifice of some cherished value; in this instance the security of our civilization.

While good and evil are thus so curiously intertwined in

history that tragic choices and dilemmas are frequent, the Christian faith is surely right in not regarding the tragic as the final element in human existence. The tragic motif is, at any rate, subordinated to the ironic one because evil and destructiveness are not regarded as the inevitable consequence of the exercise of human creativity. There is always the ideal possibility that man will break and transcend the simple harmonies and necessities of nature, and yet not be destructive. For the destructiveness in human life is primarily the consequence of exceeding, not the bounds of nature, but much more ultimate limits. The God of the Bible is, like Zeus, "jealous." But His jealousy is aroused not by the achievements of culture and civilization. Man's dominion over nature is declared to be a rightful one. Divine jealousy is aroused by man's refusal to observe the limits of his freedom. There are such limits, because man is a creature as well as creator. The limits cannot be sharply defined. Therefore, distinctions between good and evil cannot be made with absolute precision. But it is clear that the great evils of history are caused by human pretensions which are not inherent in the gift of freedom. They are a corruption of that gift. These pretensions are the source of the ironic contrasts of strength leading to weakness, of wisdom issuing in foolishness.

The Biblical view of human nature and destiny moves within the framework of irony with remarkable consistency. Adam and Eve are expelled from the Garden of Eden because the first pair allowed "the serpent" to insinuate that, if only they would defy the limits which God had set even for his most unique creature, man, they a "woe" is pronounced upon the rich for the same reason. For as wealth and power lead to pride, so weakness and poverty tend to remind men of the limits of human achievement. The ironic success which issues from the various types of failure in Biblical thought is of course not a success which is recorded in history. It belongs to a transcendent divine judgment of Him "who resisteth the proud and giveth grace to the humble." It is the symbol of the potential contradiction between all historic achievement and the final meaning of life.

2

The relevance between the Christian interpretation of ironic failures, issuing from obvious success, and our contemporary experience is obvious enough. But the Christian interpretation does not seem to fit those facets of our experience in which we are under indictment of guilt by friend and foe without just cause. That we should be less innocent as a nation than our fathers hoped; that we should be covered with guilt by assumption of the very responsibilities which express virtue; that we should become less powerful in relation to the total historical pattern as we become more powerful in given historical issues; that the happiness which our fathers regarded as the true end of life should have eluded us, all this fits very well into the pattern of ironic failure. In all of them human limitations catch up with human pretensions.

But in those ironic experiences, in which our very virtues become the occasion for mistrust against us, our history does not seem to fit into the general Christian pattern of irony. According to that pattern the poor and

would be like God. All subsequent human actions are infected with a pretentious denial of human limits. But the actions of those who are particularly wise or mighty or righteous fall under special condemnation. The builders of the Tower of Babel are scattered by a confusion of tongues because they sought to build a tower which would reach into the heavens. The possible destruction of a technical civilization, of which the "skyscraper" is a neat symbol, may become a modern analogue to the Tower of Babel.

The prophets never weary of warning both the powerful nations, and Israel, the righteous nation, of the judgment which waits on human pretension. The great nation, Babylon, is warned that its confidence in the security of its power will be refuted by history. "Thou saidst, I shall be a lady for ever . . . therefore . . . these two things shall come to thee in a moment in one day, the loss of children, and widowhood" (Isaiah 47:7, 9). They regard nothing as absolutely secure in human life and history; and believe that every desperate effort to establish security will lead to heightened insecurity. The great nation is likened unto a cedar whose boughs are higher than all other trees. This eminence tempts it to forget "that the waters made it great and the deep set it on high," which is to say that every human achievement avails itself of, but also obscures, forces of destiny beyond human contrivance. In consequence of this miscalculation Babylon will fall prey to "the terrible of the nations," to remind all the trees in the garden that they are "marked unto death." No human eminence can escape the limits of man's mortality (Ezekiel 31).

The ironic aspect of power and security being involved in weakness and insecurity by reason of stretching beyond their limits is matched by the irony of virtue turning into vice. The Pharisee is condemned and the publican preferred because the former "thanks God" that he is "not like other men." He seeks desperately but futilely to cover common human frailties by a meticulous legalism. Israel is undoubtedly a "good" nation as compared with the great nations surrounding it. But the pretensions of virtue are as offensive to God as the pretensions of power. One has the uneasy feeling that America as both a powerful nation and as a "virtuous" one is involved in ironic perils which compound the experiences of Babylon and Israel.

There is irony in the Biblical history as well as in Biblical admonitions. Christ is crucified by the priests of the purest religion of his day and by the minions of the justest, the Roman Law. The fanaticism of the priests is the fanaticism of all good men, who do not know that they are not as good as they esteem themselves. The complacence of Pilate represents the moral mediocrity of all communities, however just. They cannot distinguish between a criminal and the Saviour because each violates the laws and customs which represent some minimal order, too low for the Saviour and too high for the criminal.

The crown of irony lies in the fact that the most obvious forms of success are involved in failure on the ultimate level. "Not many wise men after the flesh, not many mighty, not many noble are called" (I Corinthians 1:26). The Saviour came "not to call the righteous but sinners

160

to repentance." He is a physician who came to minister not to them "that are whole" but to them "that are sick" (Matthew 9:12). The words are deeply ironic because "they that are whole" are obviously not healthy in his estimation precisely because they think they are. Those "who are sick" are those who know themselves to be so.

The Christian interpretation of ironic failure has its counterpart in the conception of ironic success. If the pretension of wisdom may issue in foolishness, the final wisdom, which is "withheld from the wise," may be "revealed unto babes." There may be a wholeness of view among the simple which grasps ultimate truths, not seen by the sophisticated. The "rich fool" is excoriated because he tries to gain complete security for the future; and the poor are blessed. The kingdom of heaven is likened unto a feast, invitations to which are spurned by the respectable and extended to the "maimed, the halt, and the blind" (Luke 14:15–24).

Superficially the Biblical preference for "sinners," for the poor, the foolish, the maimed, the sick, and the weak seems to be just as perverse a "transvaluation of values" as Nietzsche charged. Its justification lies in the fact that as certainly as failure may ironically issue from pride and pretension, so also may success of a high order be derived from seeming failure. The Christian faith is centered in a person who was as "the stone which the builders rejected" and who became the "head of the corner." The sick are preferred to the healthy, as the sinners are preferred to the righteous, because their lack of health prompts them to an humility which is the prerequisite of every spiritual achievement. The poor are blessed and

161

outcast, despised of their fellows, are finally exalted. We, on the other hand, are condemned by an impoverished world because we are fortunate, powerful and rich. While we are certainly not as virtuous as we pretend to be, our good fortune is not so simply a proof of our injustice as our Marxist detractors assert. What shall we make of this kind of ironic experience, in which riches rather than poverty, and power rather than weakness, have become the occasion of false judgments?

The force of these judgments against us is partly derived from a perversion of the Biblical interpretation of irony. Marxism is a secularized version of Christian apocalypse in which the beatitude, "Blessed are the poor," becomes the basis of unqualified political and moral judgments. The rich, the wise and the powerful are undoubtedly less humble than the poor, the weak and the naïve. They are, therefore, at a spiritual disadvantage in the final court of divine judgment. But this does not prove that they are morally inferior to the poor in every court of judgment. Even in the final judgment there is no guarantee that poverty will be accompanied by the virtue of humility. Significantly the two reports of this beatitude in Luke and Matthew translate the phrase which Jesus undoubtedly used, and which means "the poor of the land," differently. In the Lukan version the beatitude is rendered, "Blessed are the poor," and in the Matthean version it is "Blessed are the poor in spirit." Both versions are necessary to catch the full flavor of the beatitude. For the Lukan version alone would make poverty a guarantee of virtue, particularly of the virtue of humility, which it is not. The Matthean version alone, how-

THE IRONY OF AMERICAN HISTORY

ever, misses the "existential element." It might encourage the idea that humility of spirit is unrelated to the fortunes of life. It is related. Those who succeed in life, whether by the acquisition of power, wealth, or wisdom, do incline to value their achievements too highly and to forget the fragmentary character of all human achievements. The Matthean version alone would make the other word of Christ, "How hardly will those that are rich enter the kingdom of heaven," meaningless. It is a necessary word which emphasizes the moral hazards of success.

The Marxist religious apocalypse, on the other hand, destroys every reservation about the relation of success to virtue. It transmutes a judgment which is intended to stand as a religious warning against the pretensions of the historically successful into a simple category of historical judgment.

The poor are not actually as disinterested and pure as the Marxist apocalypse assumes. They do have fewer interests to defend than the rich. But though their justified resentments against injustice may be a creative force in history, their bitterness and their compensatory utopian visions may as frequently be sources of confusion as the social pride of the successful. Utopia is, in fact, "the ideology of the poor."* Invariably those who suffer from the arrogance or the power of others wrongfully assume that the evils from which they suffer are solely the consequence of the peculiar malice of their oppressors; and fail to recognize the root of the same evils in themselves. Thus, the intellectuals of the Orient actually engage in serious arguments on the question whether it would be

*Cf. Karl Mannheim, *Ideology and Utopia.*

164

possible for an Oriental nation to be "imperialistic." In the same way members of minority ethnic groups invariably assume that racial arrogance is a peculiar vice of the group which causes their suffering.

In the Marxist apocalypse one error is piled upon another with regard to the virtue of the poor. They are not only assumed to be completely disinterested or to have interests absolutely identical with the interests of the whole of mankind. But also no thought is given to the fact that if they become historically successful they will cease to be poor. Furthermore, the oligarchy, which presumes to speak for the poor claims to participate in their supposed sanctity. To cap the mountain of errors, the poor, to whom all virtue is ascribed, are identified with the industrial proletariat. This latter error becomes a more and more vicious source of confusion as communism seeks to conquer great peasant civilizations. One reason for the fanatic collectivization program is to be found in the communist effort to transmute peasants into industrial workers by changing farms into "grain factories."

All these errors enter into the monstrous evils of communism. It has transmuted religious truths, intended to warn against the element of pretension in all human achievements into political slogans, effective in organizing a political movement in which these very pretensions achieve a noxious virulence of unparalleled proportions. This is one reason, and perhaps the chief reason, why the communist alternative to the injustices of our civilization has universally created greater injustices and hatched more terrible tyrannies than previously known in history. Perhaps it is the crowning irony of our day that the vir-

tues of the poor should thus have become a screen of
sanctity for their not so virtuous resentments; that an
oligarchy should have found a way to harness these resentments into engines of political power; and that this
power should have been used for a program which not
only despoils the rich but also defrauds the poor.

3

Irony must be distinguished as sharply from pathos as
from tragedy. A pathetic situation is usually not as fully
in the consciousness of those who are involved in it as
a tragic one. A tragic choice is purest when it is deliberate.
But pathos is constituted of essentially meaningless cross-
purposes in life, of capricious confusions of fortune and
painful frustrations. Pathos, as such, yields no fruit of
nobility, though it is possible to transmute pathos into
beauty by the patience with which pain is borne or by
a vicarious effort to share the burdens of another. Thus,
the situation in a displaced persons camp may be essentially pathetic; but it may be shot through with both
tragedy and grace, through the nobility of victims of a
common inhumanity in bearing each other's sorrows. One
who is involved in a pathetic situation may be conscious
of the pathos without thereby dissolving it. We can, after
all, pity ourselves. But consciousness of the pathos does
not dissolve it since the participant does not bear responsibility for it. He is the victim of untoward circumstances; or he has been caught in the web of mysterious
and fateful forces in which no meaning can be discerned
and from which no escape is possible.

An ironic situation is distinguished from a pathetic

166

one by the fact that a person involved in it bears some responsibility for it. It is distinguished from a tragic one by the fact that the responsibility is not due to a conscious choice but to an unconscious weakness. Don Quixote's ironic espousal and refutation of the ideals of knight errantry may be detected by the reader whose imagination is guided by the artist-observer, Cervantes. But Don Quixote is as unconscious of the absurdity of his imitation of the ideals of chivalry as the knights are unconscious of the fraudulence of their ideals.

Elements of irony, tragedy or pathos may, of course be detected in life and history without any guiding principle of interpretation. All three types of experience are occasionally so vividly presented that they compel the observer either to the combination of pity and admiration which implies tragedy; or to the pure pity which pathos elicits; or to the laughter and understanding which are the response to irony.

But a basic faith or ultimate presupposition of meaning will determine which of these three categories is regarded as the most significant frame of meaning for the interpretation of life as a whole. If man is regarded as a noble creature who must prove his humanity primarily by "defying the trampling march of unconscious power" (Bertrand Russell), the interpretation of life becomes basically tragic. If man is regarded primarily as a prisoner of dark and capricious forces with no possibility of triumphing over the vast confusion of life the interpretation of life becomes basically pathetic.

The Christian preference for an ironic interpretation is derived not merely from its conception of the nature of human freedom, according to which man's transcendence over nature endows him with great creative possibilities which are, however, not safe against abuse and corruption. It is also derived from its faith that life has a center and source of meaning beyond the natural and social sequences which may be rationally discerned. This divine source and center must be discerned by faith because it is enveloped in mystery, though being the basis of meaning. So discerned, it yields a frame of meaning in which human freedom is real and valid and not merely tragic or illusory. But it is also recognized that man is constantly tempted to overestimate the degree of his freedom and forget that he is also a creature. Thus he becomes involved in pretensions which result in ironic refutations of his pride.

Naturally an interpretation of life which emphasizes the dire consequences of vain pretensions and sees them ironically refuted by actual experience must induce those who accept the interpretation to moderate the pretensions which create the irony. Consciousness of an ironic situation tends to dissolve it. It may be dissolved into pure despair or hatred. If, for instance, a nation should regard the accusations of injustice, which are made against it, as prompted purely by the malice of neighbor or foe; if it should fail to understand how our very confidence in our own justice may lead to unjust demands upon our friends, its mood may turn either into despair about the seeming confusion of counsel in human affairs or into hatred of the malicious accuser. An ironic smile must turn into bitter laughter or into bitterness without laughter if no covert relation is acknowledged between an unjust indictment and the facts of the case. If, on the other hand, a religious sense of an ultimate judgment upon our individual and collective actions should create an awareness of our own pretensions of wisdom, virtue or power which have helped to fashion the ironic incongruity, the irony would tend to dissolve into the experience of contrition and to an abatement of the pretensions which caused the irony. This alternative between contrition on the one hand and fury and hatred on the other hand faces nations as well as individuals. It is, in fact, the primary spiritual alternative of human existence. The question for a nation, particularly for a very powerful nation, is whether the necessary exercise of its virtue in meeting ruthlessness and the impressive nature of its power will blind it to the ambiguity of all human virtues and competencies; or whether even a nation might have some residual awareness of the larger meanings of the drama of human existence beyond and above the immediate urgencies.

The difficulties in facing this issue are threefold. In the first place nations (and, for that matter, all communities as distinguished from individuals) do not easily achieve any degree of self-transcendence, for they have only inchoate organs of self-criticism. That is why collective man always tends to be morally complacent, self-righteous and lacking in a sense of humor. This tendency is accentuated in our own day by the humorless idealism of our culture with its simple moral distinctions between good and bad nations, the good nations being those which are devoted to "liberty."

The second reason for our difficulty in sensing the

ironies in which we are involved is our encounter with a foe the fires of whose hostility are fed by an even more humorless pretension. No laughter from heaven could possibly penetrate through the liturgy of moral self-appreciation in which the religion of communism abounds. Goaded by this hostility and wounded by unjust charges it is difficult to admit any ironic ambiguity in our virtues or achievements. Thus we are tempted to meet the foe's self-righteousness with a corresponding fury of our own. The sense of a more ultimate judgment upon us is obscured by the injustice of immediate hostile judgments. This is why a frantic anti-communism can become so similar in its temper of hatefulness to communism itself, the difference in the respective creeds being unable to prevent the similarity of spirit. Therefore we must not speak too glibly about the spirit of "humanity" and "humaneness" in our civilized world. For the spirit of humanity is not preserved primarily by a correct definition of the nature of "humanitas" but rather by an existential awareness of the limits, as well as the possibilities of human power and goodness.

There is the final difficulty that involvement in the actual urgencies of history, even when men and nations are confronted with less vindictiveness than communism generates, makes the detachment, necessary for the detection of irony, difficult. Could Tolstoi have written his ironic interpretation of Napoleon's invasion of Russia at the time of that struggle? Would it have been imaginatively possible for him or tolerable for his readers? Tolstoi delighted in proving that the conscious intent of the participants in the struggle had little to do with its deeper meaning. It was, in fact, his thesis that the momentous consequences of the conflict were achieved by inadvertence rather than conscious intent. He was perhaps too scornful of the conscious purposes of the participants. "The best generals I have known," he wrote, "were stupid and absent-minded men—Napoleon Bonaparte himself. I remember his limited self-satisfied face at Austerlitz. Not only does a good army commander not need any special qualities of love, poetry, tenderness and philosophic inquiring doubt. He should be limited, firmly convinced that what he is doing is very important . . . and only then will he be a brave leader."

Yet the situation of the participant in historic struggles is not quite as desperate, spiritually, as Tolstoi assumes. We might well consider the spiritual attainments of our greatest President during our Civil War as a refutation of such pessimism. Lincoln's responsibilities precluded the luxury of the simple detachment of an irresponsible observer. Yet his brooding sense of charity was derived from a religious awareness of another dimension of meaning than that of the immediate political conflict. "Both sides," he declared, "read the same Bible and pray to the same God. The prayers of both could not be answered—that of neither has been answered fully."

Lincoln's awareness of the element of pretense in the idealism of both sides was rooted in his confidence in an over-arching providence whose purposes partly contradicted and were yet not irrelevant to the moral issues of the conflict. "The Almighty has His own purposes," he declared; but he also saw that such purposes could not annul the moral purposes of men who were "firm in the

171

right as God gives us to see the right." Slavery was to
be condemned even if it claimed divine sanction, for:
"It may seem strange that any men should dare to ask
a just God's assistance in wringing their bread from the
sweat of other men's faces." Yet even this moral condemnation of slavery is followed by the scriptural reservation:
"But let us judge not, that we be not judged."

This combination of moral resoluteness about the immediate issues with a religious awareness of another dimension of meaning and judgment must be regarded as
almost a perfect model of the difficult but not impossible
task of remaining loyal and responsible toward the moral
treasures of a free civilization on the one hand while yet
having some religious vantage point over the struggle.
Surely it was this double attitude which made the spirit
of Lincoln's, "with malice toward none; with charity for
all" possible. There can be no other basis for true charity;
for charity cannot be induced by lessons from copybook
texts. It can proceed only from a "broken spirit and a
contrite heart."

Applied to the present situation Lincoln's model would
rule out the cheap efforts which are frequently made to
find some simple moral resolution of our conflict with
communism. Modern communist tyranny is certainly as
wrong as the slavery which Lincoln opposed. We do not
solve any problem by interpreting it as a slightly more
equalitarian version of a common democracy which we
express in slightly more libertarian terms. The hope that
the conflict is no more than this and could be composed
if only we could hold a seminar on the relative merits of
equalitarian and libertarian democracy, is, in fact, an

expression of sentimental softness in a liberal culture and reveals its inability to comprehend the depth of evil to which individuals and communities may sink, particularly when they try to play the role of God to history.

Lincoln's model also rules out our effort to establish the righteousness of our cause by a monotonous reiteration of the virtues of freedom compared with the evils of tyranny. This comparison may be true enough on one level; but it offers us no insight into the corruptions of freedom on our side and it gives us no understanding of the strange attractive power of communism in a chaotic and impoverished world.

We do, to be sure, face a problem which Lincoln did not face. We cannot say, "Both sides read the same Bible and pray to the same God." We are dealing with a conflict between contending forces which have no common presuppositions. But even in this situation it is very dangerous to define the struggle as one between a God-fearing and a godless civilization. The communists are dangerous not because they are godless but because they have a god (the historical dialectic) who, or which, sanctifies their aspiration and their power as identical with the ultimate purposes of life. We, on the other, as all "God-fearing" men of all ages, are never safe against the temptation of claiming God too simply as the sanctifier of whatever we most fervently desire. Even the most "Christian" civilization and even the most pious church must be reminded that the true God can be known only where there is some awareness of a contradiction between divine and human purposes, even on the highest level of human aspirations.

173

There is, in short, even in a conflict with a foe with whom we have little in common the possibility and necessity of living in a dimension of meaning in which the urgencies of the struggle are subordinated to a sense of awe before the vastness of the historical drama in which we are jointly involved; to a sense of modesty about the virtue, wisdom and power available to us for the resolution of its perplexities; to a sense of contrition about the common human frailties and foibles which lie at the foundation of both the enemy's demonry and our vanities; and to a sense of gratitude for the divine mercies which are promised to those who humble themselves.

Strangely enough, none of the insights derived from this faith are finally contradictory to our purpose and duty of preserving our civilization. They are, in fact, prerequisites for saving it. For if we should perish, the ruthlessness of the foe would be only the secondary cause of the disaster. The primary cause would be that the strength of a giant nation was directed by eyes too blind to see all the hazards of the struggle; and the blindness would be induced not by some accident of nature or history but by hatred and vainglory.